国家哲学社会科学项目英语专业内容依托课程改革研究成果
第六届国家级优秀教学成果奖
辽宁省优秀教学成果一等奖

Understanding the U.S.A.
Physical and Human Geography

美国国情
美国自然人文地理

（第2版）

常俊跃　赵秀艳　赵永青　主编

图书在版编目(CIP)数据

美国国情：美国自然人文地理：英文 / 常俊跃，赵秀艳，赵永青主编. —2 版. —北京：北京大学出版社，2016.5
（21 世纪 CBI 内容依托系列英语教材）
ISBN 978-7-301-27111-7

Ⅰ.①美… Ⅱ.①常…②赵…③赵… Ⅲ.①英语—阅读教学—高等学校—教材②自然地理学—美国③人文地理学—美国 Ⅳ.① H319.4

中国版本图书馆 CIP 数据核字(2016)第 094941 号

书　　名	美国国情：美国自然人文地理（第 2 版） MEIGUO GUOQING: MEIGUO ZIRAN RENWEN DILI
著作责任者	常俊跃　赵秀艳　赵永青　主编
责任编辑	黄瑞明
标准书号	ISBN 978-7-301-27111-7
出版发行	北京大学出版社
地　　址	北京市海淀区成府路 205 号　100871
网　　址	http://www.pup.cn　　新浪微博：@北京大学出版社
电子信箱	zpup@pup.cn
电　　话	邮购部 62752015　发行部 62750672　编辑部 62754382
印 刷 者	北京大学印刷厂
经 销 者	新华书店
	787 毫米 × 1098 毫米　16 开本　13.25 印张　320 千字 2009 年 7 月第 1 版 2016 年 5 月第 2 版　2019 年 5 月第 3 次印刷
定　　价	39.00 元

未经许可，不得以任何方式复制或抄袭本书之部分或全部内容。
版权所有，侵权必究
举报电话：010-62752024　电子信箱：fd@pup.pku.edu.cn
图书如有印装质量问题，请与出版部联系，电话：010-62756370

编 委 会

本书主编
常俊跃　赵秀艳　赵永青

本书编校主要参与者
宋要军　张东黔　夏　洋　李莉莉　胡毓敏　曲小岑

对本项目教材开发有贡献的其他教师
宋　杰　傅　琼　刘晓蕖　霍跃红　高璐璐
黄洁芳　姚　璐　吕春媚　李文萍　范丽雅

前　言

随着我国英语教育的快速发展,英语专业长期贯彻的"以技能为导向"的课程建设理念及教学理念已经难以满足社会的需要。专家教师们密切关注的现行英语专业教育大、中、小学英语教学脱节,语言、内容教学割裂,单纯语言技能训练过多,专业内容课程不足,学科内容课程系统性差,高、低年级内容课程安排失衡及其导致的学生知识面偏窄、知识结构欠缺、思辨能力偏弱、综合素质发展不充分等问题日益凸显。

针对上述问题,大连外国语大学英语专业在内容与语言融合教学理念的指导下确定了如下改革思路:

（一）**更新语言教学理念,改革英语专业教育的课程结构**。改变传统单一的语言技能课程模式,实现内容课程与语言课程的融合,扩展学生的知识面,提高学生的语言技能。

（二）**开发课程自身潜力,同步提高专业知识和语言技能**。课程同时关注内容和语言,把内容教学和语言教学有机结合。以英语为媒介,系统教授专业内容;以专业内容为依托,在使用语言过程中提高语言技能,扩展学生的知识面,提高思辨能力。

（三）**改革教学方法,全面提高语言技能和综合素质**。依靠内容依托教学在方法上的灵活性,通过问题驱动、输出驱动等方法调动学生主动学习,把启发式、任务式、讨论式、结对子、小组活动、课堂展示、多媒体手段等行之有效的活动与学科内容教学有机结合,提高学生的语言技能,激发学生的兴趣,培养学生的自主性和创造性,提升思辨能力和综合素质。

本项改革突破了我国英语专业英语教学大纲规定的课程结构,改变了英语专业通过开设单纯的听、说、读、写、译语言技能课程提高学生语言技能的传统课程建设理念,对英语课程及教学方法进行了创新性的改革。首创了具有我国特色的英语专业内容与语言融合的课程体系;开发了适合英语专业的内容与语言融合的课程;以英语为媒介,比较系统地教授专业内容;以内容为依托,全面发展学生的语言技能;扩展学生的知识面,提高学生的综合素质,以崭新的途径实现英语专业教育的总体培养目标。

经过十年的实验探索,改革取得了鼓舞人心的结果。

（一）**构建了英语专业内容与语言融合教学的课程体系**。课程包括美国历史文化、美国自然人文地理、美国社会文化、英国历史文化、英国自然人文地理、英国社会文化、澳新加社会文化、欧洲文化、中国文化、跨文化交际、《圣经》与文化、希腊罗马神话、综合英语（美国文学经典作品）、综合英语（英国文学经典作品）、综合英语（世界文学经典作品）、综合英语（西方思想经典）、英语视听说（美国社会文化经典电影）、英语视听说（英国社会文化经典电影）、英语视听说（环球资讯）、英语视听说（专题资讯）、英语短篇小说、英语长篇小说、英语散文、英语诗歌、英语戏剧、英语词汇学、英语语言学、语言与社会、语言与文化、语言与语用等。这些课程依托专业知识内容训练学生综合运用语言的能力,扩展学生的知识面,提高学生的多元文化意识,提升学生的综合素质。

(二)系统开发了相关国家的史、地、社会文化以及跨文化交际课程资源。在内容与语言融合教学理念的指导下,开发了上述课程的资源。开发的教材改变了传统的组织模式,系统组织了教学内容,设计了新颖的栏目板块,设计的活动也丰富多样,实践教学中受到了学生的广泛欢迎。此外还开发了开设课程所需要的教学课件等。在北京大学出版社、华中科技大学出版社、北京师范大学出版社的支持下,系列教材已经陆续出版。

(三)牵动了教学手段和教学方法的改革,取得了突出的教学效果。在内容与语言融合教学理念的指导下,教师的教学理念、教学方法、教学手段得到更新。通过问题驱动、输出驱动等活动调动学生主动学习,把启发式、任务式、讨论式、结对子、小组活动、课堂展示、多媒体手段等行之有效的活动与学科内容教学有机结合,激发学生的兴趣,培养学生自主性和创造性,提高学生的语言技能,提升思辨能力和综合素质。曾有专家、教师担心取消、减少语言技能课程会对学生的语言技能发展会产生消极影响。实验数据证明,内容与语言融合教学不仅没有对学生的语言技能发展和语言知识的学习产生消极影响,而且还产生了多方面的积极影响,对专业知识的学习也产生了巨大的积极影响。

(四)提高了教师的科研意识和科研水平,取得了丰硕的教研成果。开展改革以来,团队对内容与语言融合教学问题进行了系列研究,活跃了整个教学单位的科研气氛,科研意识和科研水平也得到很大提高。课题组已经撰写研究论文60多篇,撰写博士论文3篇,在国内外学术期刊发表研究论文40多篇,撰写专著2部。

教学改革开展以来,每次成果发布都引起强烈反响。在第三届中国外语教学法国际研讨会上,与会的知名外语教育专家戴炜栋教授等对这项改革给予关注,博士生导师蔡基刚教授认为本项研究"具有导向性作用"。在第二届全国英语专业院系主任高级论坛上,研究成果得到知名专家、博士生导师王守仁教授和与会专家教授的高度评价。在中国英语教学研究会年会上,成果再次引起与会专家的强烈反响,博士生导师石坚教授等给予了高度评价。本项改革的系列成果两次获得大连外国语大学教学研究成果一等奖,两次获得辽宁省优秀教学成果奖一等奖,一次获得国家教学成果奖。目前,该项改革成果已经在全国英语专业教育领域引起广泛关注。它触及了英语专业的教学大纲,影响了课程建设的理念,引领了英语专业的教学改革,改善了教学实践,必将对未来英语专业教育的发展产生积极影响。

《美国国情:美国自然人文地理》是英语专业内容依托课程体系改革与创新这项国家级教学成果的重要组成部分,是英语专业核心必修课程基础英语所使用的教材,教材针对的学生群体是具有中学英语基础的大学生。适用于英语专业一、二年级学生,也适用于具有中学英语基础的非英语专业学生和英语爱好者学习。总体来看,本教材具备以下主要特色:

(一)遵循了全新的教学理念

经过几十年的快速发展,我国的英语教学已经出现了翻天覆地的变化。今天的英语学习者不再满足只是单词、语法、句型等等英语语言知识的学习,他们更希望读到地道的英语,在享受英语阅读乐趣的同时又能增长知识,开阔视野,了解英语国家,进而更好地运用英语与英语国家人民进行交流。本教材改变了"为学语言而学语言"的传统教材建设理念,在具有时代特色且被证明行之有效的内容依托教学理论指导下,改变了片面关注语言知识和语言技能忽视内容学习的作法。它依托学生密切关注的美国地理文化知识,结合自然人文知识内容组织学生进行语言交际活动,在语言交流中学习有意义的知识内容,既训练语言技能,也丰富相关知识,起到的是一箭双雕的作用。

(二) 涉及了系统的地理内容

《美国国情:美国自然人文地理》是一本系统关注美国自然地理和人文地理的教材。全书分为15个单元,把美国划分为东北部、东南部、中西部、西南部和西部五大地理区域,帮助读者了解美国诸州及重要城市,领略美国的山川河湖以及国家公园的美景。在介绍了美国自然地理的基础之上,还介绍了美国的人文知识:传奇的历史、有趣的传说、伟大的人物、奇异的遗址、日新月异的工农业等等。

(三) 引进了真实的教学材料

英语教材是英语学习者英语语言输入和相关知识输入的重要渠道。本教材大量使用真实、地道的语言材料,为学生提供了高质量的语言输入。此外,为了使课文内容更加充实生动,易于学生理解接受,编者在课文中穿插了大量的插图、表格、照片等真实的视觉材料,表现手段活泼,形式多种多样,效果生动直观,让读者身临其境,感同身受。

(四) 设计了新颖的教材板块

本教材每一单元的主体内容均包括 Before You Read,Start to Read,After You Read 和 Read More 四大板块,包括课前热身、课文正文、课后练习、辅助阅读、专有名词列表、娱乐园地、附录内容等。课前热身包括启发性的问题或准备活动;主课文介绍重要的自然和人文地理知识并突出显示了语言学习重点;课后练习关注美国地理知识学习和英语语言学习;辅助阅读内容对主课文进行补充,为学有余力的读者提供更加充实详细的内容;专有名词列表为读者省去了查阅美国地理专有名词的麻烦;相关网址、电影、书籍、歌曲推荐可以让读者选择自己感兴趣的内容,对美国进行多角度探索;附录内容提供了各种美国地图,介绍了各州州旗、州花、州鸟、州面积,主要城市的概况等等。教材不仅在结构上确立了学生的主体地位,而且系统的安排也方便教师借助教材有条不紊地开展教学活动。

(五) 提供了多样的训练活动

为了培养学生的语言技能和综合素质,本教材在保证历史知识体系完整的前提下,在关注英语语言知识训练和相关知识内容传授的基础上精心设计了生动多样的综合训练活动,如小组讨论、广告创意、故事接龙、对比写作等等。教材在每一单元都精心设计了旨在对学生在语法、词汇、篇章结构、语言功能等方面进行全面严格的基本技能练习。同时,编者通过参阅大量国外资料,设计出与美国自然人文地理相关的、学生参与度极高的课堂和课外活动。就连副课文都精心设计了培养寻读、略读能力的练习。多样化的活动打破了传统教材单调的训练程式,帮助教师设置真实的语言运用情境,组织富于挑战性的、具有意义的语言实践活动。它们改变了教师单纯灌输、学生被动接受的教学方式,促使学生积极思考、提问、探索、发现、批判,培养自主获得知识,发现问题和解决问题的能力,培养学生综合运用语言和知识进行沟通的能力、逻辑思维能力和探索求知的能力。

(六) 推荐了经典的学习材料

教材的另一特色在于它对教学内容的延伸和拓展。在每个章节的最后部分,编者向学生推荐经典的书目、影视作品、名诗欣赏以及英文歌曲等学习资料,这不仅有益于学生开阔视野,也使教材具有了弹性和开放性,方便不同院校不同水平学生的使用。这些活动的设置使得课堂教学得以延伸,也能激发学生的学习热情。

(七) 引进了先进的数码技术。

采用"互联网+"技术,实现从纸质资源到立体化多媒体资源的立体呈现,学习者可利用移动设备上的二维码扫描软件在线阅读相关内容和收听相关录音。

本教材是我国英语专业综合英语课程改革的一项探索,凝聚了全体编写人员的艰苦努力。然而由于水平所限,还存在疏漏和不足,希望使用本教材的老师和同学们能为我们提出意见和建议。您的指导和建议将是我们提高的动力。

编者

2016 年 5 月 17 日

于大连外国语大学

Unit 1　Panoramic View of the USA / 1
　　Text A　General Characteristics and Major Regions of the USA / 2
　　Text B　The Face of the Land / 3
　　Text C　The Rivers / 7

Unit 2　View of the Northeast / 12
　　Text A　The "Melting Pot" / 13
　　Text B　New England / 19

Unit 3　Landform of the Northeast / 23
　　Text A　Niagara Falls and the Appalachians / 24
　　Text B　Coastal Plains and Cape Cod / 25
　　Text C　More about Cape Cod / 29

Unit 4　Coastal Cities in the Northeast / 33
　　Text A　Development of the Coastal Cities / 34
　　Text B　Boston / 40

Unit 5　Important Centers of the USA in the Northeast / 44
　　Text A　The Capital City / 45
　　Text B　The Nation's Most Cosmopolitan City / 46
　　Text C　Broadway / 51

Unit 6　Land of Changes in the Southeast / 55
　　Text A　The Southeast and Its Problems / 56
　　Text B　Population of the Southeast / 61
　　Text C　The Top in the Southeast / 62

Unit 7　Touring the Southeast / 66
　　Text A　The Mighty Mississippi River and the Ozarks / 67

    Text B   Flat Plains and Islands / 69
    Text C   Memphis / 73

Unit 8   View of the Midwest / 77
    Text A   Physical Features of the Midwest / 78
    Text B   Landform of the Midwest / 79
    Text C   Mount Rushmore National Memorial / 85

Unit 9   More about the Midwest / 90
    Text A   Settlement on the Plains / 91
    Text B   The Past and Present of the Midwest / 92
    Text C   Belts in the Midwest / 98

Unit 10   The Southwestern States / 104
    Text A   Oklahoma & Texas / 105
    Text B   New Mexico & Arizona / 106
    Text C   Santa Fe, the City Different / 111

Unit 11   Landform of the Southwest / 115
    Text A   Desert and Canyon / 116
    Text B   Plateau, Rivers and Plains / 118
    Text C   Drought in the Southwest / 123

Unit 12   View of the West / 127
    Text A   The Rocky Mountains, Clear Rivers and Salty Lakes / 128
    Text B   Hottest, Driest, and Highest / 130
    Text C   Bear River Course / 133

Unit 13   Temples of Nature and Cities of the Pacific / 137
    Text A   Temples of Nature / 138
    Text B   Cities of the Pacific / 140
    Text C   Yellowstone National Park / 144

Unit 14   Newest States / 149
    Text A   Alaska / 150
    Text B   Hawaii / 155
    Text C   Hawaii, a Time Travel Dream / 158

Unit 15   Review: Regions of the USA / 164
    Text A   New England, Mid-Atlantic, Southeast and Midwest / 165
    Text B   The Southwest / 171
    Text C   The West / 173

Appendix 1　USA State Flags / 177
Appendix 2　State Capitals，Largest Cities and Name Origins / 179
Appendix 3　Fifty States，Nick Names and Fun Facts / 182
Appendix 4　States by Order of Entry into Union / 185
Appendix 5　State Birds and State Flowers / 187
Appendix 6　State Areas / 195
Appendix 7　重点参考书目和网站 / 198

Unit 1
Panoramic View of the USA

> In the United States there is more space where nobody is than where anybody is. That is what makes America what it is.
> —Gertrude Stein (1874—1946)

Unit Goals

- To have a general idea of the geography of the USA
- To be familiar with useful geographical terms about the USA
- To be able to describe the geographical features of the USA
- To be able to use the passive voice more skillfully

Before You Read

1. Tick (√) the neighboring countries and oceans of the USA.

Countries		Oceans	
China		the Pacific	
Canada		the Atlantic	
France		the Indian	
Mexico		the Arctic	

2. There are _____ states in the USA, and _____ states are contiguous.
3. Have you ever heard of "the backbone of the continent" in the USA? What is it?

4. Which of the following is the national bird of the USA?

A. European Robin

B. Red-crowned Crane

C. Kiwi

D. Bald Eagle

5. Form groups of three or four students. Try to find, on the Internet or in the library, more information about the USA which interests you. Prepare a 5-minute classroom presentation.

Start to Read

Text A General Characteristics and Major Regions of the USA

The United States is a federal constitutional republic. The country is situated mostly in central North America in the Western Hemisphere. It consists of forty-eight **contiguous** states on the North American continent, Alaska, an enormous peninsula which forms the northwestern part of North America, and Hawaii, an **archipelago** in the Pacific Ocean. It also holds several United States territories in the Pacific and the Caribbean.

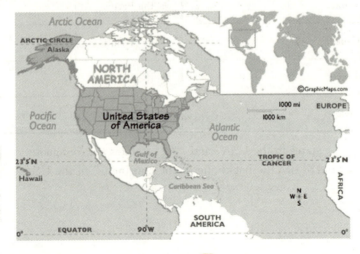

The United States shares land borders with Canada to the north and Mexico to the south, and a territorial water border with Russia in the northwest. The contiguous forty-eight states are otherwise bounded by the Pacific Ocean on the west, the Atlantic Ocean on the east, and the Gulf of Mexico on the southeast. Alaska borders the Pacific Ocean to the south, the Bering Strait to the west, and the Arctic Ocean to the north, while Hawaii lies far to the southwest of the mainland in the Pacific Ocean.

Forty-eight of the states are in the single region between Canada and Mexico; this group is referred to, with varying **precision** and **formality**, as the "continental or contiguous United States," and as the "Lower 48." Alaska, which is not included in the term "contiguous United States," is at the northwestern end of North America, separated from the Lower 48 by Canada. The State of Hawaii is an archipelago in the Pacific Ocean. The capital city, Washington, District of Columbia, is a federal district located on land **donated** by the state of Maryland. (Virginia had also donated land, but it was returned in 1847.) The United States also has overseas territories with varying levels of independence and organization.

The United States could be divided into five regions. These regions are the Northeast, the Southeast, the Midwest, the Southwest, and the West. The regions of the United States are grouped by history, traditions, economy, climate, and geography. Each region is different from one another.

Text B   The Face of the Land

On a **topographic** map of the United States, the mountains look like **jagged** masses, the plains like vast open flat spaces, and the rivers like

meandering threads. Today, highways and railways crisscross the land, making travel easy. But only a few generations ago, the topographic features on the map represented great dangers and difficulties. Today's visitors, riding over a good road in the Cascade Mountains in the west coast states of Oregon and Washington, may see marks on the rocks made by ropes where pioneer settlers painfully lowered their horses and wagons down cliffs to reach the **fertile** river valley far below. In the Sierra Nevada Mountains of California, the main route now runs through a mountain pass which was once too narrow for a wagon to go through. Pioneer families reaching that pass had to **take** their wagons **apart** piece by piece, carry them through, and then **reassemble** them on the other side.

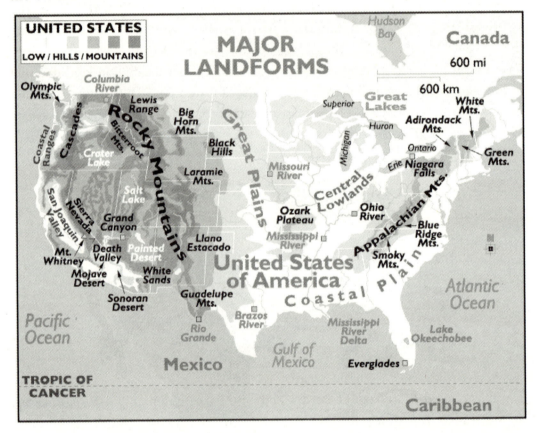

Modern means of communication and transportation have enabled man to overcome these **obstacles**. Poles and wire now carry electrical power and telephone communication over **ridges** that are so deep in snow that only persons wearing snowshoes or skis can reach them. Railroads run along the sides of mountains or in tunnels through them. Bridges have been built over valleys and rivers. Highways run through the burning heart of deserts.

Much of the geography and history of the United States was **determined** some 10,000 to 25,000 years ago. At that time, the great northern ice cap flowed over the North American continent and ground into it a number of major changes. These ice flows determined the size and **drainage** of the Great Lakes. They changed the direction of the Missouri River and carved the channel of the Hudson River. They pushed soil off a huge part of Canada into the United States, thus creating the northern part of the central agricultural basin—one of the richest farming areas in the world.

After You Read

Knowledge Focus

1. **Fill in the blanks according to the geographical knowledge you have learned in the texts above.**
   (1) The United States is a country in the _____ Hemisphere. It consists of _____ contiguous states on the North American continent, and Hawaii.
   (2) The USA shares land borders with Canada and _____ and a water border with Russia.
   (3) The contiguous forty-eight states are otherwise bounded by _____ on the west, _____ on the east, and the Gulf of Mexico on the _____.
   (4) The United States could be divided into five regions. They are the Northeast, _____, Midwest, _____, and the West.
   (5) The five Great Lakes, which the United States shares with _____, are estimated to contain about half of the world's _____.
   (6) In the east of the USA lie _____, the oldest mountains in the United States.
   (7) _____, "the backbone of the continent," are considered young mountains of the same age as _____ in Europe, _____ in Asia, and _____ in South America.
   (8) Washington, D.C., is located on land donated by _____.

2. **Write T in the brackets if the statement is true, and write F if it is false.**
   (1) The USA consists of 48 states. (   )
   (2) The USA is bordered by Australia and Canada. (   )
   (3) The Rockies, located in the west of the USA, are old mountains in the country. (   )
   (4) Alaska borders the Pacific Ocean to the south, the Bering Strait to the west, and the Arctic Ocean to the north. (   )

Language Focus

1. Fill in the blanks with the proper form of the following words or expressions you have learned in the texts.

| resemble | take...apart | enable...to |
| grind | determine | reassemble |

(1) This dictionary will _____ you _____ understand German words.

(2) Pioneer families had to _____ the wagons _____ piece by piece, carry them through, and then _____ them on the other side.

(3) He _____ his father in character as well as in appearance.

(4) The amount of the rainfall _____ the size of the crop.

(5) The great northern ice cap flowed over the North American continent and _____ into it a number of major changes.

2. Fill in the blanks with the proper forms of the words in the brackets.

(1) The topographic features on the map represented many _____ (difficult).

(2) This soil has good _____ (drain).

(3) That is when the Nile River flooded its banks, bringing water and _____ (fertile) to the land.

(4) A marked change in _____ (topographic) is a fault or deep valley.

3. Fill in the blanks with the proper prepositions or adverbs that collocate with the neighboring words.

(1) This group is referred _____ _____ the "continental or contiguous United States," and as the "Lower 48."

(2) Alaska, which is not included in the term "contiguous United States," is _____ the northwestern end of North America, separated _____ the Lower 48 by Canada.

(3) The United States also has overseas territories _____ varying levels of independence and organization.

(4) The great northern ice cap flowed over the North American continent and ground _____ it a number of major changes.

4. Correct the grammatical mistakes about the passive voice in the following sentences.

(1) The country situated mostly in central North America.

(2) The contiguous forty-eight states were bound by the Pacific Ocean on the west, the Atlantic Ocean on the east, and the Gulf of Mexico on the southeast.

(3) The group was referred to as the "continental or contiguous United States," and as the "lower 48."

(4) The regions of the USA group by history, traditions, economy, climate, and geography.

(5) Much of the geography of the USA is determined some 10,000 to 25,000 years ago.

Comprehensive Work

1. **Pair Work:** Work with your partner, and mark the following on the outline map of North America.

Canada	Mexico
Alaska	Hawaii
the Rockies	the Appalachians
the Great Lakes	the Mississippi
the Gulf of Mexico	the Sierra Nevada Mountains
the Pacific	the Atlantic

2. **Solo Work:** Write a paragraph to a foreign friend, explaining where China is situated and what it consists of.

Text C   The Rivers

Read the passage quickly, and find the information to fill in the blanks in the following statements with the help of the map.

(1) _____, called the "father of waters," flows from its northern sources in _____ to _____, which makes it one of the world's longest waterways.

(2) _____ pours into the Mississippi river from the west, coloring the river deep brown with small pieces of soil, whereas _____ joins the Mississippi from the east with waters clear and blue.

(3) All the rivers east of the Rockies finally reach _____; all the waters to the west of the Rockies finally arrive at _____. Therefore, the crests of the Rocky Mountains are known as _____.

(4) The two great rivers of the Pacific side are _____ in the south, and _____, which rises in Canada and drains the north.

(5) _____, the foremost river of the Southwest, forms a natural boundary between _____ and the United States.

The Mississippi is one of the world's great continental rivers, like the Amazon in South America, the Congo in Africa, the Volga in Europe, or the Ganges, the Amur, and the Yangtze in Asia. Its waters are gathered from two-thirds of the United States and, together with the Missouri (its chief western branch), the Mississippi flows some 6,400 kilometers from its northern sources in the Rocky Mountains to the Gulf of Mexico, which makes it one of the world's longest waterways.

The Mississippi has been called the "father of waters." Through all its lower course, it wanders along, appearing lazy and harmless. But people who know the river are not **deceived** by its **benign** appearance, for they have had many bitter struggles with its floods. Finally, they had to learn that nothing was to be gained by fighting against the **rages** of the mighty stream. To tame it, Americans have had to accept some of the river's own terms and to **undertake** the patient work of **conserving** and rebuilding soil, grasslands and forests, far back to where the waters begin to gather.

Where the Missouri pours into the Mississippi from the west, it colors the river deep brown with small pieces of soil. Farther downstream, where the clear waters of the principal eastern **tributary**, the Ohio, join the Mississippi, evidence of the difference between the dry west and rainy east becomes apparent. For kilometers, the waters of the two rivers flow on side by side, without mixing. Those from the west are brown; they have robbed the soil in areas of sparse **vegetation**. The waters from the east are clear and blue; they come from hills and valleys where plentiful forest and plant cover has kept the soil from being washed away.

Like the Mississippi, all the rivers east of the Rockies finally reach the Atlantic; all the waters to the west of the Rockies finally arrive at the Pacific. For this reason the **crests** of the Rocky Mountains are known as the Continental Divide. There are many places in the Rockies where a visitor may throw two snowballs in opposite directions and know that each will feed a different ocean.

The two great rivers of the Pacific side are the Colorado in the south, and the Columbia, which rises in Canada and drains the north. In the dry western country, both rivers, very different in character, are **vital** sources of life. Wild in prehistoric times, the Columbia cut and shaped the land, but now flows with quiet **dignity**. But the Colorado is still a river of enormous **fury**—wild, restless and angry. It races and **plunges**, cutting deeply into the desert rocks. But even the furious Colorado has been dammed and put to work. All the farms and cities of the southwestern corner of the country depend on its waters.

The Rio Grande, about 3,200 kilometers long, is the **foremost** river of the Southwest. It forms a natural boundary between Mexico and the United States, which together have built **irrigation** and flood control projects of mutual benefit.

Proper Names

Alaska 阿拉斯加州
Caribbean 加勒比海
Deccan Plateau 德干高原(印度)
Eastern Europe 东欧
Hawaii 夏威夷
Maryland 马里兰州
Mexico 墨西哥
North America 北美洲
Oregon 俄勒冈州
South America 南美洲
the Amazon 亚马孙河
the Appalachians 阿巴拉契亚山脉
the Arctic Ocean 北冰洋
the Atlantic Ocean 大西洋

the Bering Strait 白令海峡
the Cascade Mountains 卡斯科德山脉
the Central Agricultural Basin 中央农业盆地
the Central Lowland 中央低地
the Coast Ranges 沿海山脉
the Colorado Plateau 科罗拉多高原
the Colorado River 科罗拉多河
the Congo 刚果河(位于中西非,又称扎伊尔河 Zaire)
the Continental Divide 落基山脉分水岭
the District of Columbia 哥伦比亚特区
the Ganges 恒河(印度)
the Grand Canyon 大峡谷
the Great Basin 大盆地

the Great Lakes 五大湖	the Rio Grande 格兰德河
the Great Plains 大平原	the Rocky Mountains 落基山脉
the Gulf of Mexico 墨西哥湾	the Sierra Nevada Mountains 内华达山脉
the Hudson River 哈得孙河	the Volga 伏尔加河(俄罗斯)
the Mississippi River 密西西比河	Virginia 弗吉尼亚州
the Missouri River 密苏里河	Washington 华盛顿州
the Ohio River 俄亥俄河	Western Hemisphere 西半球
the Pacific Ocean 太平洋	

For Fun

Works to read
National Geographic Magazine

It is the official journal of the National Geographic Society. It published its first issue in 1888, just nine months after the Society itself was founded. It is immediately identifiable by the characteristic yellow frame that surrounds its front cover.

There are 12 monthly issues of the National Geographic per year, plus additional map supplements. On rare occasions, special editions are also issued. It contains articles about geography, popular science, history.

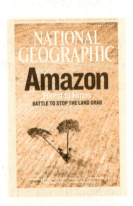

Movies to see
Once Upon a Time in America

It is a 1984 epic crime film directed by Sergio Leone, starring Robert De Niro and James Woods. The story chronicles the lives of Jewish ghetto youths who rise to prominence in New York City's world of organized crime. The film explores themes of childhood friendships, love, loss, greed, violence, the passage of time, broken relationships, and the appearance of mobsters in American society.

Songs to enjoy

"America the Beautiful" by Lee Greenwood

O beautiful for spacious skies,
For amber waves of grain,
For purple mountain majesties
Above the fruited plain!
America! America!
God shed his grace on thee
And crown thy good with brotherhood

From sea to shining sea!

O beautiful for pilgrim feet
Whose stern impassioned stress
A thoroughfare for freedom beat
Across the wilderness!
America! America!

God mend thine every flaw,
Confirm thy soul in self-control,
Thy liberty in law!

O beautiful for heroes proved
In liberating strife.
Who more than self their country loved
And mercy more than life!
America! America!
May God thy gold refine
Till all success be nobleness

And every gain divine!

O beautiful for patriot dream
That sees beyond the years
Thine alabaster cities gleam
Undimmed by human tears!
America! America!
God shed his grace on thee
And crown thy good with brotherhood
From sea to shining sea!

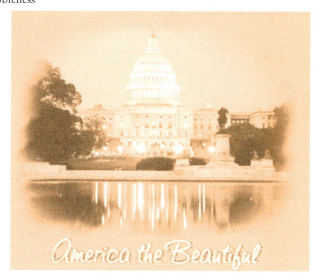
America the Beautiful

O beautiful for halcyon skies,
For amber waves of grain,
For purple mountain majesties
Above the enameled plain!
America! America!
God shed his grace on thee
Till souls wax fair as earth and air
And music-hearted sea!

O beautiful for pilgrims' feet,
Whose stern impassioned stress
A thoroughfare for freedom beat
Across the wilderness!
America! America!
God shed his grace on thee
Till paths be wrought through
wilds of thought
By pilgrim foot and knee!

O beautiful for glory-tale
Of liberating strife
When once and twice,
for man's avail
Men lavished precious life!
America! America!
God shed his grace on thee
Till selfish gain no longer stain
The banner of the free!

O beautiful for patriot dream
That sees beyond the years
Thine alabaster cities gleam
Undimmed by human tears!
America! America!
God shed his grace on thee
Till nobler men keep once again
Thy whiter jubilee!

Unit 2
View of the Northeast

> We like to have a melting pot of cultures...
> —Jim Huffstetler

Unit Goals

- To have a general idea of the states in the Northeast
- To be familiar with the geographical terms concerning the Northeast
- To be able to describe the features of the Northeast
- To be able to explain the effect of the wilderness upon the colonists in the Northeast
- To be able to use restrictive attributive clauses more skillfully

Before You Read

1. Match the flowers with their names and the states.

Rose　　　　　　Purple Lilac　　　　Peach Blossom

Delaware　　　　New Hampshire　　　New York

2. What is a melting pot? Why is the Northeast called the "melting pot"?
3. Which city in the Northeast of the USA is the oldest steel industrial center of the country?
4. Is New York a city or a state?
5. Have you ever heard of "New England"? Is it a part of England?
6. Form groups of three or four students. Try to find, on the Internet or in the library, more information about the agriculture and industry of the Northeast. Prepare a 5-minute classroom presentation.

Start to Read

Text A   The "Melting Pot"

The Northeast region of the USA consists of the states of Maryland, Delaware, New Jersey, Pennsylvania, New York, Connecticut, Rhode Island, Massachusetts, Vermont, New Hampshire, Maine, and the nation's capital, the District of Columbia. That sounds like many places, but all these states and the District of Columbia put together are not nearly as big as the lone state of Texas!

The Northeast is the part of the United States which most visitors see, and the part that is most often described. The skyscrapers of New York, the steel mills of Pittsburgh—these symbols of industrial America belong to this region.

Into this area of industry came millions of Europeans who made of it what became known as the "melting pot," the **fusion** of people from many nations into Americans. More than any other part of the country, this section reflects European culture and tradition.

When we see this great area today, it is hard to realize that it was **wilderness** only three centuries ago. The effect of the wilderness upon the colonists was a powerful force in developing the United States. As soon as **permanent** settlements were made in the new land, subtle changes occurred in the people. Faced with the problems of a new and uncharted land, these settlers had to give up many of the traditional behavior patterns of Europe. In order to survive, they developed a **cooperative** and **democratic** life-style that laid the foundations of the American political system and **pragmatic** philosophy.

Even today, the visitor who expects only factories, apartment houses, and crowded streets is surprised. In the Northeast, he sees more **wooded** hills than factory chimneys, more fields than concrete roads, more farmhouses than office buildings.

The features of the land over most of this region are **on a small and gentle scale**. It is a country of many brooks, of low mountain ridges, of rolling hills, of orchards, pastures and vegetable gardens. In only a few places is a visitor so much as 40 kilometers distant from rich farms. There are areas of true wilderness such as the forests in the northern part of the State of Maine, where to this day the only way of crossing great stretches of land or water is by foot or **canoe**. Everywhere, the outer reaches of cities **mingle** with farms, and in many towns there are old farmhouses and barns, which have been changed into **dwellings**, and now they are crowded close by taller buildings.

The **observant** visitor quickly guesses that he is in a relatively old farming region on which a pattern of cities and industries has grown and spread. What he cannot see is how the look of the countryside has changed with this growth of industry. A few generations ago, the majority of these farms produced grain to be sold, and a variety of plants, meats and **poultry** for the farm family itself. Today, most of the farms are developed **primarily** to one type of farming: dairy cattle, or vegetables, or chickens, or fruit. Most **specialize** in products that can be rushed fresh to the cities nearby. Thus, the nature of agricultural production has changed to meet the needs of the region's industrial economy.

This change in agricultural production **illustrates** a very important factor in American geography: the "market." In economic-geographic **terminology**, the market means all the people and organizations in an area that are able to buy goods. And, in examining the industries of the USA Northeast, we find that many of them are there because the area is a good market, because there is an industrial and agricultural population **financially** able to buy clothing, goods, equipment and services. The manufacturers of these items find it cheaper to bring in **raw** materials and produce these goods near a large market than to ship the finished items and arrange their sale from a distance. Furthermore, when these industries are established in the market area, more workers are employed, thus further adding to its economy.

After You Read

Knowledge Focus

1. **Fill in the blanks according to the geographical knowledge you have learned in the text above.**
   (1) The Northeast region consists of 11 states and the nation's capital, _____.
   (2) _____ is the oldest steel industrial center of the USA.
   (3) Known as the "melting pot," the Northeast of the USA reflects _____ culture and traditions.
   (4) The Northeast was _____ only three centuries ago, the effect of which upon the colonists was a powerful force in developing the USA.
   (5) There are areas of true wilderness in the Northeast, such as the forests on the northern part of the state of _____, where to this day the only way of crossing great stretches of land or water is by foot or canoe.
   (6) In the Northeast, the nature of _____ production has changed to meet the needs of the region's industrial economy.
   (7) In economic-geographic terminology, the _____ means all the people and organizations in an area that are able to buy good.
   (8) The Northeast is a good market because there is an _____ and _____ population financially able to buy clothing, goods, equipment and services.

2. **Write T in the brackets if the statement is true, and write F if it is false.**
   (1) New York City is located in New York State in the Northeast of the USA. (　)
   (2) The Northeast of the USA is a region of more than 11 states, which makes it larger than Texas, the second largest state in the USA. (　)
   (3) The District of Columbia is a famous city, located in New York State. (　)
   (4) New York City is famous for its skyscrapers. (　)
   (5) Pittsburgh is well-known as the car capital of the USA. (　)
   (6) Maine is the most northeastern state of the USA. (　)
   (7) Both Rhode Island and Long Island are the states in the Northeast of the USA. (　)
   (8) In the Northeast, visitors can see factories, apartment houses, crowded streets and wooded hills and farmhouses as well. (　)

Language Focus

1. Fill in the blanks with the proper forms of the following expressions you have learned in the text.

belong to	be faced with	on a small scale	
mingle with	change into	specialize in	give up
lay the foundation of	add to	the majority of	

(1) The features of the land are _____.

(2) Today, most farms _____ products that can be quickly transported to the cities nearby.

(3) The newly-established industries _____ the economy of the area.

(4) _____ the difficulties of a new land, the settlers had to work hard.

(5) The life-style adopted by the European settlers _____ the American politics and philosophy.

(6) These symbols of industrial America _____ the northeast of the USA.

(7) The outer reaches of cities _____ farms, so a visitor would always feel surprised to see more hills and fields in the northeast of the USA.

(8) People _____ the old farmhouses and barns _____ dwellings a few decades ago.

(9) The settlers _____ their traditional patterns, developing a democratic life-style.

(10) _____ the settlers came from the European countries.

2. Fill in the blanks with the proper forms of the words in the brackets.

(1) The automobile _____ (assemble) lines of Detroit is one of the symbols of _____ (industry) America.

(2) In the Northeast of the USA, a visitor sees more _____ (wood) hills than _____ (crowd) streets.

(3) In order to survive after the _____ (settle), the _____ (settle) developed a _____ (cooperate) and _____ (democracy) life-style.

(4) There are areas of true _____ (wild) such as the forests in the northern part of the State of Maine.

(5) Today, most of the farms are devoted _____ (primary) to one type of farming.

(6) In the Northeast of the United States, there is an _____ (industry) and _____ (agriculture) population _____ (finance) able to buy clothing, goods, equipment and services.

(7) The USA, especially its northeast, is known as the "melting pot," the _____ (fuse) of people from many countries into Americans.

3. Fill in the blanks with the proper prepositions and adverbs that collocate with the neighboring words.

(1) The Northeast of the USA consists _____ 11 states and the nation's capital city.

(2) The geographical terms of the region sound _____ many places.
(3) Millions of Europeans made _____ the Northeast what became known _____ the "melting pot."
(4) These people had to give _____ many _____ the traditional behavior patterns of Europe.
(5) The effect of the wilderness _____ the colonists was a powerful force in developing the USA.
(6) In only a few places is a visitor so much _____ 40 kilometers distant from rich farms.
(7) The manufacturers of these items find it cheaper to bring _____ raw materials and produce these goods near a large market _____ to ship the finished items and arrange their sale from a distance.

4. Correct the grammatical mistakes about the restrictive attributive clauses in the following sentences.
(1) The Northeast is the part of the USA in which most visitors see, and the part that is most often described.
(2) In order to survive, they developed a cooperative and democratic lifestyle laid the foundations of the American political system and pragmatic philosophy.
(3) The observant visitor quickly guesses that he is in a relatively old farming region which a pattern of cities and industries have grown and spread.
(4) Most specialize in products that can rush fresh to the cities nearby.
(5) In economic-geographic terminology, the market means all the people and organizations in an area which are able to buy goods.
(6) In the Sierra Nevada Mountains of California, the main route now runs through a mountain pass which once too narrow for a wagon to go through.
(7) Poles and wire now carry electrical power and telephone communication over ridges that is so deep in snow that only persons wearing snowshoes or skies can reach them.

Comprehensive Work

1. Group Work: Work in groups of four or five. Suppose you are ad writers who work for a state in the Northeast America. Your assignment is to write an advertisement to be printed on a page of a newspaper to get people to move to or visit your state. You want to tell the good things about your state and explain why people should visit or move there. You can use *Unit 2 View of the Northeast*, the Internet, and other resources to learn more about the state you have chosen.
  1. Our state: _____
  2. Natural wonders of our state: _____

  3. Landmarks, historical places, and museums in our state: _____

  4. Special foods or cultural attractions in our state: _____

5. Who would want to move there and why? Fishermen? Scientists?
_____

6. Possible things to include in our ad:
   A map of _____
   Photos of _____
   Drawings or cartoons of _____

7. Show a brief sketch of what your ad might look like.

2. **Pair Work**: Work with your partner and locate and label, on the map below, the states in the Northeast and the nation's capital, the District of Columbia.

Unit 2 View of the Northeast

Read More

Text B   New England

Read the passage quickly and answer the following questions.
(1) Which of the following is NOT part of New England?
   A. Main.   B. Vermont.   C. Maryland.
(2) _____ were the earliest European settlers of New England.
(3) The top-ranking educational institutions of the USA DO NOT include _____.
   A. Yale   B. Harvard   C. Oxford

New England is one of the two major regions of the northeast United States comprising the modern-day states of Maine, New Hampshire, Vermont, Massachusetts, Connecticut, and Rhode Island. This region is perhaps the best-defined one of the USA, with more uniformity and more of a shared **heritage** than other regions of the country. New England has played a **dominant** role in American history. From the late 17th century to the mid of the late 18th century, New England was the nation's cultural leader in political, educational, cultural and intellectual thought. During this time, it was the country's economic center.

The earliest European settlers of New England were English Protestants who came in search of religious liberty. They gave the region its distinctive political format—town meetings (an outgrowth of meetings held by church elders), in which citizens gathered to discuss issues of the day. Town meetings still function in many New England communities today and have been revived as a form of dialogue in the national political arena.

Education is another of the region's strongest **legacies**. The cluster of top-ranking universities and colleges in New England—including four of the eight schools of the Ivy League, as well as MIT, Tufts, and numerous other **elite** colleges and universities—is unequaled by any other region. America's first college, Harvard, was founded at Cambridge, Massachusetts in 1636. Many of the graduates from these schools end up settling in the region after school, providing the area with a well educated populace and its most valuable resource, the area being relatively lacking in natural resources, besides "ice, rocks, and fish." True to their enterprising nature, New Englanders have used their brains to make up the gap; for instance, in the 19th century, they made money off their frozen pond water, by shipping ice in fast clipper ships to tropical locations before **refrigeration** was invented.

As some of the original New England settlers migrated westward, immigrants from Canada, Ireland, Italy, and Eastern Europe moved into the region. Despite a changing population, New England maintains a distinct cultural identity. It can be seen in the simple woodframe houses and **quaint** white church steeples that are features of many small towns, and in the traditional lighthouses that dot the Atlantic coast. New England is also well known for its **mercurial** weather, its crisp chill, and **vibrantly** colored **foliage** in autumn. The region is a popular tourist destination. As a whole, the area of New England tends to be liberal in its politics, albeit restrained in its personal mores. Because the area is the closest in the United States to England, the region often shows a greater **receptivity** to European ideas and culture in relation to the rest of the country.

Proper Names

Baltimore 巴尔的摩(马里兰州第一大城市)
Cambridge 剑桥(美国麻省一城镇)
Connecticut 康涅狄格州
Delaware 特拉华州
Eastern Europe 东欧
Harvard 哈佛
Ireland 爱尔兰
Italy 意大利
Maine 缅因州
Maryland 马里兰州
Massachusetts 马萨诸塞州(简称麻省)
MIT (Massachusetts Institute of Technology) 麻省理工学院

New England 新英格兰(美国大陆东北角六州)
New Hampshire 新罕布什尔州
New Jersey 新泽西州
New York 纽约州
New York City 纽约市
Oxford (University) 牛津大学(英国)
Pennsylvania 宾夕法尼亚州
Philadelphia 费城(宾夕法尼亚州第一大城市)
Pittsburgh 匹兹堡(宾夕法尼亚州第二大城市)
Rhode Island 罗得岛州
the American Revolution 美国革命
the Chesapeake Bay 切萨皮克湾
the Continental Congress 大陆议会

the Delaware River 特拉华河
the District of Columbia 哥伦比亚特区
the Declaration of Independence 独立宣言
the English Catholics 英国天主教徒
the English Protestants 英国清教徒
the Friends (Quakers) 教友派信徒
the Ivy League 常青藤联盟

the Mid-Atlantic 中大西洋地区
the Northeast 美国东北部
the US Constitution 美国宪法
Tufts 塔夫茨大学
Vermont 佛蒙特州
Yale 耶鲁

Websites to visit

http://www.regentsprep.org/Regents/ushisgov/themes/immigration/theories.htm

This is a page about "Melting Pot" Theory and "Salad Bowl" Theory.

Movies to see

United 93

On September 11, 2001, four young Arabians prepared themselves for hijacking United Flight 93. The same day, America witnessed three attacks, as one plane destroyed the Pentagon and two others, destroyed both towers of the World Trade Center. The FAA and Military are unprepared for this. A delay of United 93 allows the passengers to learn of the attacks, which leads them to believe that they too are part of a hijacking and must stop the terrorists in order to save thousands of lives.

Songs to enjoy

"Melting Pot" by Boyzone

Take a pinch of white man
Wrap it up in black skin
Add a touch of blue blood
And a little bitty bit of red Indian boy

Curly black and kinky
Oriental sexy
If you lump it altogether
Well you've got a recipe for a get along scene…

Oh what a beautiful dream
If it could only come true
You know, you know...

What we need is a great big melting pot
Big enough to take the world and all it's got
Keep it stirring for a hundred years or more
Turning out coffee colored people by the score
Yeah...no

Rabbis and the friars
Bishops and the gurus
We had The Beatles and The Sun Gods

a long time ago (it's true)
But then it really didn't matter what religion you choose
Oh no no nooo

Mick and Lady Faithful
Lord and Missus Graceful
You know the living could be tasteful
Why don't we all get together in a loving machine
I'd better call up the Queen
It's only fair that she know
You know, you know...

Unit 3

Landform of the Northeast

> The lakes represent a fresh water ecosystem that's unique on our planet, supporting thousands of species, including human beings.
> —Jim Doyle

Unit Goals

- To have a general idea of the land of the Northeast
- To be able to describe the landform of the Northeast
- To be able to explain how Niagara Falls and Cape Cod were formed
- To be able to use more skillfully the present participles as adverbial

 Before You Read

1. Which one of the following is a cape, and which one is a peninsula?

  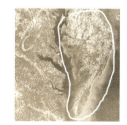

2. Which one of the following is a cod? What are the other two?

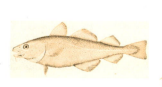 

3. Can you guess the reason why Cape Cod is so named? And how about Delmarva

Peninsula?
4. Where are the Great Lakes? What are their respective names?
5. Have you ever heard of Niagara Falls? Where are they?
6. Form groups of three or four students. Try to find, on the Internet or in the library, more information about the landforms or the tourist attractions in the Northeast. Prepare a 5-minute classroom presentation.

Start to Read

Text A Niagara Falls and the Appalachians

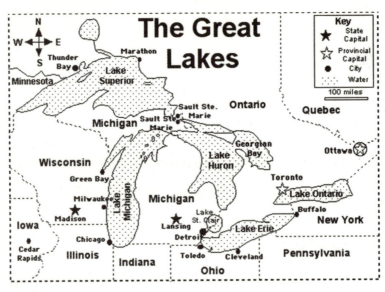

The Great Lakes are the largest group of freshwater lakes in the world. They are the giant **puddles** formed when glaciers melted years ago as the climate **warmed up**. The lakes serve as a natural border between the United States and Canada. Lake Erie and Lake Ontario are connected by the Niagara River which is not good for going rafting on. The river **plunges** over a cliff, and crashes down over 170 feet, forming the world-famous Niagara Falls. Niagara Falls is really three falls: the American Falls, the Veil of the Bride Falls on the New York side and the great big Horseshoe Falls on the Canadian side. It is a scenic spot attracting thousands of visitors

every year. Your can ride in the Maid of the Mist, a boat that explores the **gorge** below the falls, riding through the mist that rises from the falls.

Besides the water, here also lie the mountains The Appalachian Mountains are a very old landform. 250 million years ago, they were towering, **snow-capped** peaks. As time passes by, the mountains are eroded, or worn down, by wind, rain, and glacier.

The Appalachian Trail is the longest footpath in the United States, stretching 2,100 miles all along the Appalachian Mountains. It is the favorite for those who like exploring wild places. Hiking the whole trail from Maine to Georgia takes months, but it is enjoyable. Sometimes, wild turkeys, **raccoons**, **possums**, and black bear add to the excitement of the explorers along the trail.

Text B　　Coastal Plains and Cape Cod

Out of the Appalachian mountains flow some of the streams. They become waterfalls, forming the fall line which stretches from southern New York to Alabama. At the fall line, higher land suddenly drops down to the flat coastal plain, the Atlantic Coastal Plain. The fall line used to be a great source of water power for running machinery. Today, the waterfalls are used for making electric power.

Delaware, Maryland and Virginia make up the Delmarva Peninsula which is almost 300 by 100 km or about 180 by 60 miles. The ground is wet here. This land is a marsh in the Blackwater National Wildlife Refuge. Tall grasses grow everywhere and deer hide in the few clumps of trees. The wetlands are also home to ducks, geese, and even **bald** eagles, serving as a winter resort for about one million birds.

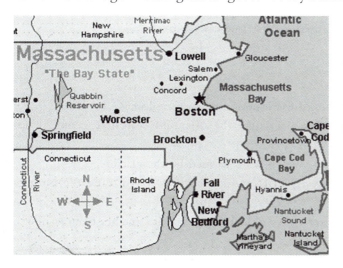

Do you know where the name Delmarva comes from? Cut the word up, and you will find it out.

How about this name—

Cape Cod? Cod is a fish, but Cape Cod is not a fish called cod. It is a part of the coastline sticking out into the big rough-and-tumble Atlantic Ocean which we call cape. All of Cape Cod was bulldozed here by a giant glacier which covered most of the Northeast with ice about a mile thick. The glacier moved slowly south, pushing everything along with it. The glacier stopped and melted when it got here, leaving a pile of dirt and rocks behind. That is how Cape Cod was formed.

 Cape Cod in the easternmost portion of Massachusetts has wide beaches and beautiful sand dunes with the smell of the salt air and the sound of the waves crashing, attracting families from all over the Northeast for their vacations.

After You Read

Knowledge Focus

1. **Fill in the blanks according to the geographical knowledge you have learned in the texts above.**
   (1) Lake Erie and Lake Ontario are connected by _____, a river not for going rafting on, since it plunges over cliffs and crashes down 170 feet. _____ is really two falls. On the New York side is _____; over the Canadian side is _____.
   (2) _____ is the favorite place for those who like exploring the wild places, since it is the longest footpath in the USA. It goes along _____, the oldest mountains in the USA.
   (3) Delmarva Peninsula is made up by Delaware, _____, and _____.
   (4) Cape Cod stands out into the _____ Ocean.
   (5) Cape Cod got there because of a giant _____.
   (6) _____ form the natural border between Canada and the USA.
   (7) A _____ is a part of the coastline that sticks out into the sea.
   (8) A peninsula is land that has _____ on three sides.

3. **Write T in the brackets if the statement is true and write F if it is false.**
   (1) Cape Cod was formed because of the eruption of some volcanos. ( )
   (2) Cape Cod is not a good vacation spot, since the Atlantic Ocean here is rough-and-tumble. ( )
   (3) The Great Lakes are five lakes, which were formed by the glaciers. ( )
   (4) The Niagara River plunges over a cliff and crashes down, forming the Niagara Falls. ( )
   (5) The Appalachian Mountains are a very old landform and it stretches from Maine to Georgia. ( )

(6) The Appalachian Trail is the longest path in the world for the animals, such as wild turkeys, raccoons, possums, and even black bears. (   )
(7) The fall line is a tourist attraction, where tourists can test their courage by jumping from high. (   )
(8) Delmarva is a state near Maryland and Virginia. (   )

Language Focus

1. **Fill in the blanks with the proper forms of the following words or expressions you have learned in the texts.**

in vain	warm up	make up	cut...up
snow-capped	stick out	wear...down	run cover

(1) All the work of the Philadelphia canal was _____.
(2) A cape is a part of the coastline that _____ into the sea.
(3) The Appalachians were young, towering and _____ peaks 250 million years ago.
(4) The glaciers melted, when the climate began to _____.
(5) _____ the word _____, and you will find out where the name comes from.
(6) Today the Appalachians are eroded, or _____, by wind, rain, and of course glaciers.
(7) The glaciers _____ most of the Northeast with ice about a mile thick.
(8) The three states _____ a peninsula.
(9) Some factories use the power to _____ machinery.

2. **Fill in the blanks with the proper forms of the words in the brackets.**
(1) Cape Cod is a _____ (favor) vacation spot for families all over the Northeast.
(2) Tourists love its _____ (width) beaches and _____ (beauty) sand dunes.
(3) The Great Lakes form a _____ (nature) border between them.
(4) Lake Erie and Lake Ontario are _____ (connection) by the Niagara River.
(5) 250,000,000 years ago, the Appalachians were young and _____ (tower) peaks.
(6) At the fall line, higher land _____ (sudden) drops down to the Atlantic _____ (coast) Plain.

3. **Fill in the blanks with the appropriate prepositions and adverbs that collocate with the neighboring words.**
(1) The glacier left a pile _____ dirt and rocks _____.
(2) The Niagara River is not a river for going rafting _____.
(3) _____ the New York side is the American Falls.
(4) There is much to see and do _____ Niagara Falls.
(5) Tourists can ride in the Maid of the Mist, a boat that explores the gorge _____ the falls.
(6) The fall line stretches _____ southern New York _____ Alabama.

(7) Today, their waterfalls are used _____ making electric power.

(8) _____ one million birds spend the winter in the Blackwater National Wildlife Refuge.

4. **Change the following two sentences in each item into one by using the present participles.**

(1) The river plunges over a cliff, and crashes down over 170 feet. It has formed the world-famous Niagara Falls.

(2) You can ride in the Maid of the Mist, a boat that explores the gorge below the falls. The boat rides through the mist that rises from the falls.

(3) The Appalachian Trail is the longest footpath in the USA. It stretches 2,100 miles all along the Appalachian Mountains.

(4) They become waterfalls. They have formed the fall line which stretches from southern New York to Alabama.

(5) The wetlands are also home to ducks, geese, and even bald eagles. They have served as a winter resort for about one million birds.

(6) The glacier moved slowly south. It pushed everything along with it.

(7) The glacier stopped and melted when it got here. It left a pile of dirt and rocks behind it.

(8) Cape Cod has wide beaches and beautiful sand dunes. It has attracted families from all over the Northeast for their vacation.

Comprehensive Work

1. **Solo Work**: The words below are from the texts. Each word has something to do with the natural resources of the Northeast. Write a meaning for each word in the boxes. Include a sketch for each word to help you remember its meaning. Use *Landform of the Northeast*, a dictionary, or any other resources available to you.

trail	cape
glacier	gorge
peninsula	waterfall

2. **Pair Work**: Discuss the following questions with your partners.
   (1) What rivers or lakes are there in your hometown? What do they look like? How important are they?
   (2) Are there any mountains or hills in your hometown? Do you like them? Why or why not?

Read More

Text C   More about Cape Cod

Read the passage quickly and finish the following multiple-choice questions.

(1) Cape Cod was NOT formed _____.
   A. in the last Ice Age
   B. more than a hundred centuries ago
   C. in 11000 BC

(2) Cape Cod was named so because _____.
   A. people around liked eating codfish
   B. there were a great number of codfish
   C. it shaped like a cod

(3) Which one of the following is NOT true?
   A. Cape Cod is historical.
   B. Tourists come here for history and spectacular features as well.
   C. Today, tourists can see gulls open the clam by dropping it onto some boulder.

(4) Which one is NOT the spectacular feature of Cape Cod National seashore?
   A. It has great wall of cliffs.
   B. It has eight square miles of the dunes.
   C. It is on the Atlantic Coast.

Cape Cod National Seashore is unique. It not only provides many **recreational** opportunities, but also reveals a chapter of New England history dating from the Pilgrims to the space age.

Cape Cod is a peninsula that stands farther out to sea than any other **portion** of the Atlantic coast. It was created, geologists say, by glaciers, which dropped **deposits** here in the last Ice Age, about 11,000 years ago. It was then molded for more than a hundred centuries by winds, waves, tides and currents. Mile after mile of glacier deposits were sliced by the elements into clean-sloping cliffs. One could even pick up pebbles there brought by glaciers from the Laurentian Mountains in Canada.

After reaching out thirty-five miles into the Atlantic, Cape Cod narrows and curves **abruptly** to the north for thirty-five miles more. So it has the sea on one side and a great bay on the other. In 1602, an English navigator found **fabulous** quantities of codfish in this place thus named it Cape Cod. In 1616, Capt. John Smith said that this cape was "in the form of a sickle."

This "sickle" reeks with stories. At Follins Pond there is evidence that Norsemen visited the Cape 1,100 years ago, and Indians were living here at least 2,000 years before that. It is here that the Pilgrims first came ashore, had the first **glimpse** of the New world, first drank New World fresh water, first glimpsed the Indians, and found their first seed corn. While their ship lay in the harbor inside the Cape, they drew up the Mayflower Compact.

But most visitors do not come here to study history. They come to enjoy the delights of the Cape Cod National Seashore, to swim, to lie on the sand, to listen to the surf, to hunt and fish, to dig clams, to watch birds, or to comb the beaches for shells, rocks, driftwood and other treasures.

The charm of Cape Cod lies not in **spectacular** sights, but rather in the subtle beauty of the marshes, with their flat islands, winding streams, blue herons, and herring gulls. Hundreds of thousands of birds use the Atlantic flyway in the Cape Cod area, so **diligent** bird watchers can spot 250 different species during the year. On the flats shorebirds feed and nest on the beaches. In summer, terns nest on the beaches, and, in winter, major concentrations of waterfowl are found just off-shore and in the marshes.

An interesting sight when the tide is low is a herring gull flying along forty feet up, a clam held tightly in its hooked bill, looking for a suitable boulder. In the past, gulls opened the clam by dropping it onto some **boulder**, but now they **concentrate** on an easier task—the national seashore's large paved parking areas. Sections near the marshes are **sprinkled** with clamshell bits.

Nevertheless, Cape Cod National Seashore does have two spectacular features. One is the **magnificent** wall of cliffs, sixty to seventy feet high, where the Cape's tablelands meet the Atlantic. People tell tall tales about this place. If you stand on the bank here and throw pieces of wood over the bank, the winds will blow them back. The famous Henry David Thoreau once recorded that "boys and men amuse themselves by running and trying to jump off the bank with their jackets opened, and being blown back."

North of these **impressive** cliffs are eight square miles of the most spectacular dunes on the Atlantic Coast. The building material came from the highlands to the south—**gnawed** out of the cliffs by wind and wave, carried for miles by ocean currents, then stopped here. They were then shaped, and

shifted by centuries of winds. People who have braved this wilderness during the winter when the northwest winds blow report that dunes can change shape in an hour. Some are free-moving; others are stabilized with beach grass and low-growing **dwarf-like** trees.

Since 1602 fishing has played a major part in the life of the Cape's people. In the year it was named Cape Cod, Provincetown, Truro, and Wellfleet became well-known whaling centers, while Cape Cod square-riggers carried American Products around the world. To guide them, five lighthouses were built within the present boundaries of the seashore.

People are flocking to the Cape Cod National Seashore in increasing numbers, because here on this historic peninsula with its shining sands, its rolling dunes, its woodlands and its ever-changing seascape is the answer to what so many city-bred Americans seek—the peace and content of the **unspoilt** outdoors.

Proper Names

Alabama 阿拉巴马州
Cape Cod 科德角（麻省最东端）
Cape Cod National Seashore 科德角国家海岸
Capt. John Smith 约翰·史密斯船长
Follins Pond 弗林斯·旁得湖
Georgia 佐治亚州
Henry David Thoreau 亨利·大卫·梭罗（美国著名作家，实用主义哲学家）
Indians 印第安人
Lake Erie 伊利湖
Lake Huron 休伦湖
Lake Michigan 密歇根湖
Lake Ontario 安大略湖
Lake Superior 苏必利尔湖
Niagara Falls 尼亚加拉大瀑布
Norsemen 诺斯曼人（北欧人）
Provincetown 普罗文斯敦（麻省科德角一城镇）
the American Falls 亚美利加瀑布
the Appalachian Mountains 阿巴拉契亚山
the Appalachian Trail 阿巴拉契亚山道
the Atlantic Coast 大西洋海岸

the Atlantic Coastal Plain 大西洋沿岸平原
the Atlantic Ocean 大西洋
the Blackwater National Wildlife Refuge 黑水国家野生保护区（马里兰州东岸）
the Delmarva Peninsula 德尔马瓦半岛（美国大西洋沿岸平原一部分）
the Horseshoe Falls 霍斯舒瀑布
the Ice Age 冰河时代
the Laurentian Mountains 洛朗山区（加拿大魁北克南部一山脉）
the Maid of the Mist 雾中少女号轮船
the Mayflower Compact 五月花号公约
the New World 新世界（指西半球，尤指南北美洲及其附近岛屿）
the Niagara River 尼亚加拉河
the Pilgrims 1620年移居美洲的英国清教徒
the Space Age 太空时代（1957年人类发射第一颗人造卫星至今）
Truro 特鲁罗（麻省一城镇）
Wellfleet 韦尔费利特（麻省一城镇）

For Fun

Websites to visit

http://www.on.ec.gc.ca/greatlakes/For_Kids-WS4DB7BBAD-1_En.htm

   This is a website that offers fun stuff and Great Lakes information.

http://www.tourismniagara.com/

   This is a website that gives visitors suggestions on what to see, where to stay, etc., in the Niagara region.

Movies to see

Niagara

   As two couples are visiting Niagara Falls, tensions between one wife and her husband reach the level of murder.

Poems to enjoy

Cataracts cascading
Sun shining
Mist mounting
Rainbows arching

Rapids roaring
Gulls soaring
Blossoms blooming
People peering

Picture making
Breath taking
World wonder
Niagara Fall

(by Betty J. Beam, 2001)

Music to enjoy

"Appalachian Spring" by Aaron Copland

   Aaron Copland's "Appalachian Spring" captures the essence of an ideal America, one of open fields and endless possibilities. It is one of the most inspiring and symbolic works of the century.

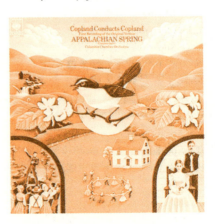

Unit 4
Coastal Cities in the Northeast

> The opening of the Erie Canal to New York in 1825 stimulated other cities on the Atlantic seaboard to put themselves into closer commercial touch with the West.
>
> —John Moody

Unit Goals

- To be acquainted with the importance of the sea to the Northeast
- To have a general idea about the development of New York City, Philadelphia, Baltimore and Boston
- To be able to describe how the coastal cities in the Northeast developed
- To be able to use past perfect tense properly

Before You Read

1. Can you find New York City, Philadelphia, Baltimore and Boston on the map of the USA?
2. What do you think of their geographic positions?
3. Have you ever heard of the Erie Canal? And why is it so important?
4. Do you know the first railroad across the mountains? Where was it?

5. Can you match the pictures with the cities, and the cities with their states?

    New York City   Philadelphia   Boston

    Pennsylvania   Massachusetts   New York State

6. Form groups of three or four students. Try to find, on the Internet or in the library, more interesting information about Boston, Baltimore and Philadelphia. Prepare a 5-minute classroom presentation.

Start to Read

Text A   Development of the Coastal Cities

    The sea means many things to the industrial Northeast. From the outer point of Long Island northward, the coast **borders** one of the world's great "fish bowls," an area especially rich in the tiny plants and animals that support a large fish life. Along this coast there are several busy fishing ports, many little fishing villages, and the small towns from which American sailing ships used to **depart**, seeking whales. In the days before petroleum, when whale oil was used on factory wheels and **fueled** lamps, these sailing ships hunted whales all around the world.

    The sea also means long **stretches** of jagged rock and gleaming white beaches to which millions of city people go on summer holidays. And from the earliest days of the American settlements, the sea has meant foreign trade. The young nation depended heavily on its overseas trade which brought to North America many of the items not yet produced there: cloth, tools and **furnishings**.

Today, four of the most heavily populated areas in the northeast are centered around the seaports of Boston, New York, Philadelphia and Baltimore. These four places are not only important ports, but leading industrial centers.

The importance of these northeastern cities, both as ports and as **hubs** of manufacturing, did not simply **come about by chance**.

About 1815, when the westward settlement of the United States had already become an important movement, trade routes from the ports to the **interior** began to be a serious problem. The slow wagon trains of that time, drawn by horses or oxen, were too expensive for moving freight any great distance. One answer to the transportation problem was a canal, an idea that was especially practical in New York State. From the eastern end of Lake Erie all the way across the state to the Hudson River, there is a long **strip** of low land. The Hudson itself flows deep and without waterfalls to New York harbor. For the small population and the agricultural economy of the time, constructing so long a waterway was a most **ambitious** project, but—after several years of work—the Erie Canal was completed in 1825. Freight costs from New York City to Lake Erie were immediately **cut to** about one-tenth of what they had been, and New York, which had **previously** been smaller than Philadelphia and Boston, quickly became the leading city of the coast. When, in the years which followed, traffic on the Great Lakes was joined to that on the Mississippi River, New York became the **terminal** of a great inland shipping system that extended from the Atlantic far up the western branches of the Mississippi. The coming of the railroads made canal shipping less important, but it tied New York even more closely to the interior.

Exports from New York were greater than imports. Consequently, shipping companies, on the return trip from Europe, were willing to carry passengers for very low fares. Thus, New York also became the greatest port for the **entry** of immigrants.

While the Erie Canal was being built, the people of Philadelphia began to worry about the future of their own port. Unlike New York, they had no easy canal route over one river system to the interior. Mountains **barred** the way either to the Great Lakes or to the Ohio River, the eastern branch of the Mississippi. Nevertheless, the people of Philadelphia built a canal. Where it reached the ridges that separated the eastern slopes from those to the west, railroad tracks came to the edge of the canal, and **hoists** lifted the **barges** onto special railroad cars, to be carried over the mountains. Philadelphia's canal was one of the major engineering feats of the 19th century America, but all the work was in **vain**. Shipping on the Erie Canal was so much cheaper that Philadelphia's effort was little used. But the Philadelphians swallowed their disappointment and looked about for a better plan. Since coal had been discovered near several upper tributaries of the Delaware River, canals were built to the mines. This project worked. The **combination** of the port with cheap shipping for fuel assured Philadelphia a position as a manufacturing center. Later, railroads provided the much-needed link with the interior.

The fear that their port would lose its importance also worried the people of Baltimore. Their city is situated where the hard rocks of the Appalachian hills and the soft soil of the coast come together. This made waterfalls, and the waterpower gave them an early advantage for manufacturing. But they realized that this was not advantageous enough, and conditions were not right for building a canal. Instead, they constructed the first railroad across the mountains, and it became a vital center for export and import trading. Yearly, about 6,000 **vessels** move into Baltimore's natural harbor. **Lumber**, ores, **crude** oil—raw materials from the world—are unloaded and reshipped by rail or coastal tank ship to American industry in exchange for grain and machinery. World trade helps make Baltimore America's sixth largest port.

Boston alone, of these four ports, did not develop **primarily** through export trade. Located in a region which early became an important center of industry and, therefore, required raw materials, Boston was primarily an import point and only secondarily an export city for the northeastern corner of the country.

After You Read

Knowledge Focus

1. Write T in the brackets if the statement is true and write F if it is false.

(1) The Erie Canal was very successful in linking New York with the interior and

cutting down the freight. ( )
(2) Philadelphia's canal was as successful as the Erie Canal. ( )
(3) The people of Baltimore constructed the first railroad across the mountains. ( )
(4) Boston, like New York, Philadelphia and Baltimore, developed primarily through export trade. ( )
(5) New England is located in the Northwestern corner of the country. ( )
(6) The Erie Canal made New York the leading city of the coast though it had previously been smaller than Philadelphia and Boston. ( )
(7) The Hudson River played an important role in New York City's development. ( )
(8) The people in Baltimore had an early advantage of waterpower for manufacturing. ( )

2. **Match the facts with the coastal cites in the Northeast America.**

New York   a vital center for export and import trading
                  exports greater than imports
Philadelphia   primarily an import point
                  a manufacturing center
Baltimore   the Erie canal
                  the greatest port for immigrants
Boston   the canals built to the mines

3. **Discuss the following questions with your partner.**
   (1) In which states are New York, Boston, Philadelphia and Baltimore respectively? Compare their positions and the possible advantages.
   (2) Why was a canal a good and practical answer to the transportation problem in New York State?
   (3) Which cities in China are comparable to New York, Boston and Philadelphia? And why?

Language Focus

1. **Fill in the blanks with the proper form of the following expressions you have learned in the text.**

| come about | in exchange for | in vain | join...to |
| cut...to | by chance | be rich in | be centered around |

(1) The coast northward borders one of the "fish bowls," an area especially _____ the tiny plants and animals that support a large fish life.
(2) Can you explain how it _____ that the four cities were not only important ports, but leading industrial centers?
(3) The work of the Philadelphia canal was _____.
(4) In Baltimore's natural harbor, raw materials from the world are unloaded and reshipped by rail or coastal tank ship to American industry _____ grain and

machinery.

(5) The completion of Erie Canal _____ freight costs from New York City to Lake Erie _____ about one-tenth of what they had been.

(6) The sea cities did not flourish simply _____.

(7) In the following years, traffic on the Great Lakes was _____ that on the Mississippi River.

(8) Today some heavily populated areas in the northeast _____ the seaports.

2. **Fill in the blanks with the proper forms of the words in the brackets.**

(1) For the small population and the economy of the time, constructing the Erie Canal, so long a waterway, was a most _____ (ambition) project.

(2) New York became the greatest port for the _____ (enter) of immigrants.

(3) These sea cities are heavily _____ (population) areas in the Northeast.

(4) The Philadelphians swallowed their _____ (disappointed) caused by the unsuccessful canal.

(5) New York developed great export trade. _____ (consequence), shipping companies were _____ (will) to carry _____ (pass) for low fares on the _____ (return) trip.

(6) Boston was _____ (primary) an import point and only _____ (second) an export city for the _____ (northeast) corner of the country.

(7) The overseas trade brought to North America such items as cloth, tools and _____ (furnish).

(8) The _____ (combine) of the port with cheap shipping for fuel assured Philadelphia a position as a manufacturing center.

3. **Fill in the blanks with the proper prepositions and adverbs that collocate with the neighboring words.**

(1) One answer _____ the transportation problem was a canal.

(2) The railroads tied New York even more closely _____ the interior.

(3) Shipping companies, _____ the return trip from Europe, were willing to carry passengers for very low fares.

(4) All the work they did in the past few weeks was _____ vain.

(5) Railroads provided the much-needed link _____ the interior.

(6) Since coal had been discovered near several upper tributaries of the Delaware River, canals were built _____ the mines.

(7) Conditions here were not right _____ building a canal.

(8) Lumber, ores, crude oil—raw materials _____ the world—are unloaded and reshipped _____ rail or coastal tank ship to American industry.

4. **Discuss with your partner whether the past perfect tense in the following sentences is used properly and why (or why not).**

(1) From the earliest days of the American settlement, the sea **had meant** foreign trade.

(2) About 1815, when the westward settlement of the USA **had already become** an

important movement, trade routes from the ports to the interior began to be a serious problem.

(3) Constructing so long a waterway was a most ambitious project, but after several years of work, the Erie Canal **had been completed** in 1825.

(4) Freight costs from New York City to Lake Erie were immediately cut to about one-tenth of what they **had been**.

(5) New York, which **had previously been** smaller than Philadelphia and Boston, quickly **became** the leading city.

(6) Since coal **had been** discovered near several upper tributaries of the Delaware River, Canals were built to the mines.

Comprehensive Work

1. **Group Work**: Form groups of four or five students. Compare the roles of the Erie Canal and the Beijing-Hangzhou Canal. Identify the similarities and differences, and then report it to the class.

Canal \ Comparison	Similarities	Differences
Erie Canal		
Beijing-Hangzhou Canal		

2. **Solo Work**: Following the successes of New York, Philadelphia and Baltimore, write an article for *China Daily* or *The 21st Century* introducing the development of your hometown.

3. **Group Work**: Discuss the following questions in groups of three or four and write down the key words or phrases.

Where are the Great Lakes and the Erie Canal? And are they important to the regional and national development?

Location

The Great Lakes   The Erie Canal
_____   _____
_____   _____

Importance

The Great Lakes   The Erie Canal
a. _____   a. _____
b. _____   b. _____
c. _____   c. _____
d. _____   d. _____
...

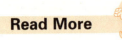

Text B　　Boston

Read the passage quickly and finish the following multiple-choice questions.

(1) Boston is NOT _____.
  A. the capital of the Commonwealth of Massachusetts
  B. the largest city in the Northeast
  C. the 21st largest city in the USA

(2) _____ did not happen in Boston.
  A. The American Revolution
  B. The Boston Massacre
  C. The Boston Tea Party

(3) What Mark Twain wrote about Boston in the third paragraph means _____.
  A. in Boston, people want to know how much you know
  B. in Boston, people values knowledge
  C. in Boston, people do not trust you

(4) Which of the following is NOT true?
  A. Boston is a center of higher education and a center for medicine.
  B. The city's economy is also based on research, finance, and technology.
  C. Boston ranks first in the country ahead of New York City and Washington D.C.

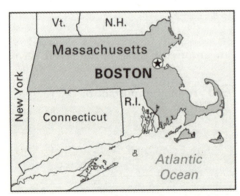

Boston is the capital and largest city of the Commonwealth of Massachusetts, and is one of the oldest cities in the United States. The largest city in New England, Boston is considered the economic and cultural center of the region, and is sometimes regarded as the unofficial "Capital of New England." Boston city proper had an estimated population of 608,352 in 2007, making it the twenty-first largest in the country.

In 1630, Puritan colonists from England founded the city on the Shawmut Peninsula. During the late eighteenth century, Boston was the location of several major events during the American Revolution, including the Boston Massacre and the Boston Tea Party. Several early battles of the American Revolution, such as the Battle of Bunker Hill and the Siege of Boston, occurred within the city and surrounding areas. Through land **reclamation** and municipal **annexation**, Boston has expanded beyond the peninsula. After American independence was attained, Boston became a major shipping port and manufacturing center, and its rich history now attracts 16.3 million visitors annually. The city was the  site of several firsts, including America's first public school, Boston Latin School (1635), and first college, Harvard College (1636), in neighboring Cambridge. Boston was also home to the first subway system in the United States.

Many consider Boston a highly cultured city, perhaps as a result of its intellectual reputation. Mark Twain once wrote of it. In New York they ask, "How much money does he have?" In Philadelphia, they ask, "Who were his parents?" In Boston they ask, "How much does he know?" Much of Boston's culture originates at its universities.

With many colleges and universities within the city and surrounding area, Boston is a center of higher education and a center for medicine. The city's economy is also based on research, finance, and technology—principally biotechnology. Boston ranks first in the country in jobs per square mile ahead of New York City and Washington D.C. The city has been experiencing **gentrification** and has one of the highest costs of living in the United States, though it remains high on world livability rankings.

Proper Names

Benjamin Franklin 本杰明·富兰克林(美国科学家、政治家、文学家和航海家)
Boston 波士顿
Boston Latin School 波士顿拉丁学校
City of Brotherly Love 友爱之城
Harvard College 哈佛学院
John Moody 约翰·穆迪
Long Island 长岛
Mark Twain 马克·吐温(美国著名作家)
North America 北美洲
Philadelphia County 费城郡
Philly 费城昵称
the Appalachian Hills 阿巴拉契亚山脉

the Battle of Bunker Hill 邦克山之战
the Boston Massacre 波士顿大屠杀
the Boston Tea Party 波士顿倾茶党
the British Empire 大英帝国
the Commonwealth of Massachusetts 马萨诸塞联邦
the Delaware River 特拉华河
the Erie Canal 伊利运河
the Nielsen Media Research 尼尔森媒介研究
the Philadelphians 费城人
the Shawmut Peninsula 邵穆特半岛(波士顿所在的半岛)
the Siege of Boston 波士顿包围战
Washington D.C. 华盛顿哥伦比亚特区

For Fun

Websites to visit

http://en.wikipedia.org/wiki/Benjamin_Franklin

　　This is a webpage on Benjamin Franklin, the famous man, who was born in Boston, Massachusetts, and did great work in Philadelphia, Pennsylvania.

http://www.ci.baltimore.md.us/

　　This is a comprehensive website about Baltimore.

http://www.boston.com/

　　This is a comprehensive website about Boston.

http://www.gophila.com/

　　This is an official visitor website for greater Philadelphia.

Movies to see

Philadelphia

　　When a man with AIDS is fired by a conservative law firm because of his condition, he hires a homophobic small time lawyer as the only willing advocate for a wrongful dismissal suit.

Songs to enjoy

"Streets of Philadelphia" by Bruce Springsteen

I was bruised and battered and I couldn't tell
What I felt
I was unrecognizable to myself
I saw my reflection in a window I didn't know
My own face
Oh brother are you gonna leave me
Wastin' away
On the streets of Philadelphia

I walked the avenue till my legs felt like stone
I heard the voices of friends vanished and gone
At night I could hear the blood in my veins
Black and whispering as the rain
On the streets of Philadelphia

Ain't no angel gonna greet me
It's just you and I my friend
My clothes don't fit me no more

Unit 4 Coastal Cities in the Northeast

I walked a thousand miles
Just to slip the skin

The night has fallen, I'm lyin' awake

I can feel myself fading away
So receive me brother with your faithless kiss
Or will we leave each other alone like this
On the streets of Philadelphia

Unit 5
Important Centers of the USA in the Northeast

> Nobody in Washington can survive if he's not political.
> —Allan Meltzer
>
> Each man reads his own meaning into New York.
> —Meyer Berger

Unit Goals

- To have a general idea about the political, financial and cultural centers of the USA in the Northeast: Washington, D.C. and New York City
- To be familiar with the geographical terms about Washington, D.C. and New York City
- To be able to introduce the famous buildings in Washington, D.C. and New York City
- To be able to explain different usages of v-ing forms

Before You Read

1. _____ is the capital of the USA. It is the _____ (political/economic) center of the USA. It is located in the _____ of the USA.
2. _____ is the spiritual and economic center of the USA. It is located in _____ state.
3. Write the names of the following buildings or monuments in the brackets and the cities they are located in on the lines.

(   ) _____   (   ) _____

Unit 5 Important Centers of the USA in the Northeast

(   )   (   )   (   )
_____   _____   _____

4. Match the proper nouns with the expressions in the right column.

        Broadway   (1) an intersection, site of annual celebration of New Year's Eve
          Harlem   (2) a street in Manhattan famous for its theaters
    Times Square   (3) the government building where the USA. Senate and the
                            House of Representatives meet
          Capitol   (4) a district of Manhattan; now largely a Black ghetto

5. Form groups of three or four students. Try to find, on the Internet or in the library, more information about Washington, D.C. and New York City, which interests you. Prepare a 5-minute classroom presentation.

Start to Read

Text A The Capital City

The capital of the United States is Washington, D.C., District of Columbia. It is where the President of the United States and about 250,000 government employees work.

The city is located at the **confluence** of the Potomac and Anacostia rivers and is flanked on the north, east, and southeast

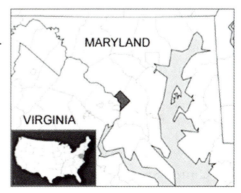

by Maryland and on the southwest by Virginia. Although the city has retained some aspects of its southern origin, it has assumed a much more cosmopolitan character. At the same time, the city struggles with social and economic **disparity**, and a number of its residential neighborhoods suffer from poverty and crime. It is hot and humid in the summer and cold and damp in the winter. The average daily temperature range is -3° to 6°C (27° to 42°F) in January and 22° to 31°C (71° to 89°F) in July. The city averages 980 mm of precipitation per year.

Washington is home to many famous and interesting public buildings and monuments, such as Washington Monument, Lincoln Memorial, Arlington National Cemetery, Thomas Jefferson Memorial, and Vietnam Veterans Memorial. The Capitol and the Supreme Court Building are also in Washington. The former is a place where members of Congress pass laws and the latter is the place where the nine judges of the Supreme Court decide if the laws are fair.

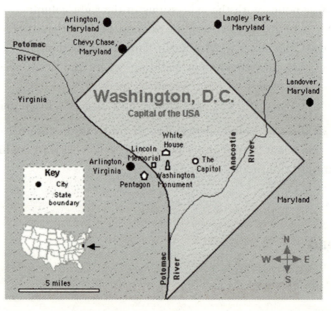

Washington is also **appealing** to tourists. About five million people visit the nation's capital every year! They eat in restaurants, stay in hotels, and buy souvenirs, contributing to the development of tourist industry which is important to the economy of Washington, D.C.

Text B The Nation's Most Cosmopolitan City

New York City (officially The City of New York) is the largest city in the United States, with its metropolitan area ranking among the largest urban areas in the world. Founded as a commercial trading post by the Dutch in 1624, it served as the capital of the United States from 1785 until 1790, and has been the nation's largest city since 1790. Located on a natural harbor, New York **exerts** global influence in commerce and finance as well as arts and entertainment. The city is an important center for international affairs, hosting the headquarters of the United Nations.

The city has many renowned landmarks. The Statue of Liberty greeted millions of immigrants as they came to America in the late 19th and early 20th centuries. Wall Street, in Lower Manhattan, has been a dominant global financial center since World War II and is home to the New York Stock Exchange. The city has been home to several of the tallest buildings in the world, including the Empire State Building and the twin towers of the former World Trade Center.

New York is the birthplace of cultural movements, including the Harlem Renaissance in literature and visual art, abstract expressionism (also known as the New York School) in painting, and hip hop, punk, salsa, and Tin Pan Alley in music. It is also the home of Broadway theater.

In 2005, nearly 170 languages were spoken in the city and 36% of its population was born outside the United States. With its 24-hour subway and constant bustling of traffic and people, New York is sometimes called "The City That Never Sleeps." Other nicknames include "Gotham" and the "Big Apple."

New York City comprises five boroughs: the Bronx, Brooklyn, Manhattan, Queens, and Staten Island. With an estimated population of 8,274,527 residents within an area of 304.8 square miles (789.43km^2), New York City is the most densely populated major city in the United States.

After You Read

Knowledge Focus

1. Fill in the blanks according to the geographical knowledge you have learned in the texts above.

(1) _____ is the Capital of the USA. The D.C. stands for _____.

(2) Washington D.C. is flanked on the north, east, and southeast by _____ and on the southwest by _____.

(3) There is _____, where members of congress pass laws, and _____, where the nine judges decide if the laws are fair.

(4) _____ is the largest city in the United States.

(5) The New York city is an important center for international affairs, hosting the headquarters of the _____.

(6) _____, in Lower Manhattan, has been a dominant global financial center since World War II and is home to the New York Stock Exchange.

(7) New York is the birthplace of cultural movements, including the _____ in literature and visual art, _____ (also known as the New York School) in painting.

(8) The City of New York comprises five boroughs, which are: the Bronx, Brooklyn, _____, _____, and Staten Island.

2. Write T in the brackets if the statement is true and write F if it is false.

(1) The President of the United States works and lives in New York. ( )

(2) The capital of the United States struggles with social and economic disparity, and a number of its residential neighborhoods suffer from poverty and crime. ( )

(3) Washington is home to many famous and interesting public buildings and monuments, such as the Statue of Liberty, Washington Monument, Lincoln Memorial, Arlington National Cemetery, Thomas Jefferson Memorial, and Vietnam Veterans Memorial. ( )

(4) In Washington, you will see many tourists. The tourist industry is the most important to the economy of Washington, D.C. ( )

(5) Founded as a commercial trading post by the Dutch in 1624, New York City has served as the capital of the United States ever since 1785, and has been the nation's largest city since 1790. ( )

(6) The city has been home to several of the tallest buildings in the world, including the Empire State Building and the twin towers of the former World Trade Center. ( )

(7) The famous Broadway Theater is located in New York City. ( )

(8) "The City That Never Sleeps," "Gotham" and the "Big Apple" are the nicknames of New York City. ( )

Language Focus

1. **Fill in the blanks with the proper form of the following words you have learned in the texts.**

confluence	flank	retain	assume
exert	renown	comprise	densely

   (1) He _____ all his influence to make them accept his plan.
   (2) Two small boys and a dog _____ the street entertainer's only audience.
   (3) The city is located at the _____ of the Blue Nile and the White Nile.
   (4) We _____ the original fireplace when we decorated the room.
   (5) New York City is the most _____ populated major city in the United Sates.
   (6) The garden is _____ to the north with large maple trees.
   (7) The problem is beginning to _____ massive proportions.
   (8) The City of New York has many _____ landmarks.

2. **Fill in the blanks with the proper forms of the words in the brackets.**

   (1) He is the most promising _____ (president) candidate.
   (2) The theory is based on a series of wrong _____ (assume).
   (3) Every girl wants to marry a _____ (million).
   (4) Right now, he is doing a _____ (commerce) course at the local college.
   (5) The company is in great _____ (finance) difficulties.
   (6) _____ (Expression) is a style of painting, music, drama, film, etc which tries to express the artist's or writer's emotional experience rather than to show the physical world in a realistic way.
   (7) What is the population _____ (dense) of this city?
   (8) The _____ (urban) of the rural area is still in progress.

3. **Fill in the blanks with the proper prepositions or adverbs that collocate with the neighboring words.**

   (1) Thousands _____ men and women work _____ television, radio, and newspaper in Washington, D.C.
   (2) The tourist industry is important _____ the economy of Washington, D.C.
   (3) Broadway is known _____ its theaters.
   (4) The D.C. stands _____ the District of Columbia.
   (5) The Capitol is where members _____ Congress pass laws.
   (6) Broadway is the longest, busiest, and one _____ the oldest main streets in the whole country.
   (7) Founded _____ a commercial trading post by the Dutch in 1624, New York City served as the capital of the United States from 1785 until 1790.
   (8) The city has been home _____ several of the tallest buildings in the world, including the Empire State Building and the twin towers of the former World Trade Center.

4. **Please discuss the usage of the v-ing forms in the following sentences with your partner.**
   (1) Washington is home to many famous **interesting** public buildings.
   (2) Washington is also **appealing** to tourists.
   (3) New York City is the largest city in the US with its metropolitan area **ranking** among the largest urban areas in the world.
   (4) Founded as a commercial **trading** post by the Dutch in 1624, it served as the capital of the US from 1785 until 1790.
   (5) New York is an important center for international affairs, **hosting** the headquarters of the US.
   (6) New York has been home to several of the tallest buildings in the world, **including** the Empire State Building and twin towers of the former World Trade Center.
   (7) With its 24-hour subway and constant **bustling** of traffic and people, New York is sometimes called "The City That Never Sleeps."

Comprehensive Work

1. **Pair Work**: Discuss the following questions with your partner and write down the key words.
   What culture in New York City is most impressive? What about Washington, D.C.? And which city do you want to visit more? Why?

New York City	Washington, D.C.
_____	_____
_____	_____
_____	_____
_____	_____

   The City you want to visit more: _____
   The reason: _____
   _____
   _____

2. **Group Work**: Work in groups of three or four students. Discuss the following questions with your group members, and summarize your points of view in diagram form.
   (1) Which cities in China do you think can more or less match Washington, D.C. and New York City in the USA?
   (2) In what ways do they resemble and differ from each other?

3. **Pair Work**: Discuss the following quote with your partner.
   "We like to think of New York as the nation's most cosmopolitan city, a place in which the independence and freedom and values of art and culture are not questioned by anybody, [as if] that debate is over. But that debate is never really over, and Ground Zero is the perfect way to bring that debate back to the fore, even in New York." —*Paul Goldberger*

(1) What is Ground Zero?
(2) What does it mean to New York?
(3) Surf the Internet for some information about the new World Trade Center and write an essay about 150 words, introducing its location, size and outlook, etc.

Read More

Text C   **Broadway**

Read the passage quickly and discuss the following questions with your partner.
(1) Why is Broadway so famous?
(2) What do the underlined sentences mean?

Broadway used to be a trail carved into the brush land of Manhattan by its Native Americans, snaking through swamps and rocks along the length of Manhattan Island. After years of development, it has become the longest, busiest, and one of the oldest main streets in the whole country.

When the Yankees win the World Series, they **parade** up Broadway. When soldiers come home from war, they parade up Broadway, too. And Broadway is where the ball drops on New Year's Eve. The big bright signs make the middle of the night as bright as day. The many theaters around here also add to the bright lights.

A stretch of Broadway is famous as the pinnacle of the American theater industry. But not only do actors and directors work in the theater, but behind the curtain, people work on costumes, makeup, lights, and sets also. Many people work to make a Broadway Show, creating a splendor for Broadway and New York as well!

Proper Names

Arlington National Cemetery 阿林顿国家公墓
Broadway 百老汇
Brooklyn 布鲁克林区
Chicago 芝加哥(美国第三大城市,位于伊利诺伊州)
Columbia Heights 哥伦比亚高地
Expansion Magazine《扩展杂志》
Fannie Mae 联邦抵押协会
Fortune 500 Companies《财富》500 强企业
George Washington 乔治·华盛顿(美国第一任总统)
Georgetown University 乔治敦大学
Gotham 哥特镇,愚人村(美国纽约市的别名)
Harlem 哈莱姆区(又译"哈林",美国纽约市曼哈顿的一个社区,曾经长期是 20 世纪美国黑人文化与商业中心,也是犯罪与贫困的主要中心)
Howard University 霍华德大学
Lincoln Memorial 林肯纪念堂
Logan Circle 洛根广场
Lower Manhattan 南曼哈顿
Mississippi 密西西比州
Manhattan 曼哈顿区
Native Americans 美国土著人
Paris 巴黎
Queens 皇后区
Staten Island 斯塔腾岛
Shaw 肖(地名)
the Anacostia River 阿纳卡斯蒂亚河
the Big Apple 大苹果(纽约俗称)
the Bronx 布朗克斯区
the Capitol 国会大厦
the City That Never Sleeps 不夜城(美国纽约市的别名)
the District of Columbia 哥伦比亚特区
the Dutch 荷兰人
the Empire State Building 帝国大厦
the Forbes《财富》(福布斯)杂志
the 14th Street Corridor 第 14 街走廊
the George Washington University 乔治·华盛顿大学
the Green Line 贝鲁特的敌我分界线
the Harlem Renaissance 哈莱姆文艺复兴
the New York School 纽约学派(抽象表现主义)
the New York Stock Exchange 纽约证券交易所
the Potomac River 波托马克河
the Statue of Liberty 自由女神像
the Supreme Court 最高法院
the Twin Towers 双子大楼
the United Nations 联合国
the U Street Corridor 美国 U 街走廊
the World Series 世界职业棒球大赛
the Yankees 美国人
Thomas Jefferson Memorial 杰斐逊纪念堂
Times Square 时代广场
Tin Pan Alley 流行歌曲出版界
Vietnam Veterans Memorial 越战纪念碑
Wall Street 华尔街
Washington, D.C. 华盛顿哥伦比亚特区
Washington Hospital Center 华盛顿医院中心
Washington Monument 华盛顿纪念碑
World Trade Center 世贸中心
World War II 第二次世界大战

For Fun

Websites to visit

http://nycgo.com/

This is a comprehensive website about New York City, on which you can get all kinds of information, including hotels, dinning, shopping, nightlife, etc.

http://www.broadway.com/

This is a comprehensive website about Broadway, on which you can find the shows on, buy tickets, watch videos and read the features.

http://www.zkenglish.com/Article/2008/461.html

This is a Chinese webpage about the famous buildings in or near Washington, D.C.

Movies to see

Sleepless in Seattle

Sam Baldwin, a Chicago architect, has lost his wife (Carey Lowell) to cancer. He and his young son Jonah move to Seattle, Washington to make a fresh start, but Sam is still disconsolate. On Christmas evening, Jonah calls into a national radio advice show and persuades his father to go on the air with him to talk about how much he misses his wife. Thousands of women around the country, touched by Sam's story, send him letters. One letter is from Annie Reed, a journalist from Baltimore, Maryland, engaged to a nice but sneeze-prone man named  Walter (Bill Pullman) who feels that there is something missing. Jonah, who has been working his way through the flood of mail, finds Annie's missive and likes that it mentions the Baltimore Orioles. He tries to convince his father to go to **New York City** to meet her on Valentine's Day, but Sam loses his temper and refuses. Jonah flies to New York and takes a taxi to **the Empire State Building**, saying he's going to meet his new mother. Sam, in pursuit, catches up with Jonah, who has not found Annie because she is busy breaking up with her fiancé. Jonah and Sam get on the down elevator just before a late Annie rushes in, but with the help of a lost backpack and teddy bear, they finally meet and all ends well.

The Broadway Melody

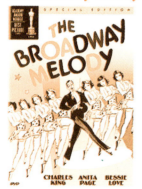

The plot involves the romances of musical comedy stars, set against the backstage hubbub of a Broadway revue. Anita Page and Bessie Love play a vaudeville sister act who have come to New York for their big break on Broadway. Charles King plays the song-and-dance man whose affection for one sister (Harriet alias Hank) is supplanted by his growing love for the younger, more beautiful sister (Queenie). Queenie tries to protect her sister and derail the love triangle by dating a wealthy but unscrupulous "stage door Johnny."

Songs to enjoy

"New York City" by Emigrate

I am lost in a world of lights
Mesmerize my nights
The sky scrapes on building sites
So I'm feelin' so alive

Whatever is clever
Whatever is clever will have to wait

Thinking on the world as large
The city's got it all
Culture clash and sidewalk trash
Don't look you might fall

And now we just feel like energy
New York City will never sleep

And now we just feel like synergy
New York City is the place to be!

I'm gonna win, I'm gonna lose
I'm gonna chase it till the end
And if you're walkin' in my shoes
You gonna make it or pretend

Whatever's clever
Whatever's clever will have to wait

And now we just feel like energy
New York City will never sleep
And now we just feel like synergy
New York City is the place to be!

Unit 6
Land of Changes in the Southeast

> What's right about America is that although we have a mess of problems, we have great capacity—intellect and resources—to do something about them.
>
> —Henry Ford

Unit Goals

- To have a general idea of the states in the Southeast
- To be able to explain the problems of the Southeast
- To be able to describe the kind of geography of the Southeast
- To be able to describe the landscapes of special beauty in the Southeast
- To be able to use comparative degree more skillfully

Before You Read

1. What is the name of the highlighted region on the map?
2. What kind of climate do you think the Southeast of the USA has?
3. Here are some photos of the fruits grown in Florida in the Southeast of the USA. Do you know their Chinese names? Can you match the following English names in the brackets with the fruits?
(carambola, dragon fruit, coconut, lychee, logan, papaya)

( )　　　　　　　　( )

( )　　　　　　　　( )

( )　　　　　　　　( )

4. Form groups of three or four students. Try to find, on the Internet or in the library, more information about the economy of the Southeast of the USA which interests you. Prepare a 5-minute classroom presentation.

Start to Read

Text A　　The Southeast and Its Problems

The Southeast of the USA comprises the states of Kentucky, West Virginia, Virginia, Tennessee, North Carolina, South Carolina, Georgia, Alabama, Mississippi, Louisiana, Arkansas, and Florida. This southeastern region is changing more rapidly than any other part of the United States—not because the land is new, but because the area's old, **exhausted** land is being given a new life.

Unit 6 *Land of Changes in the Southeast*

The problems of the Southeast area are best illustrated by a story that goes back a decade before the turn of the last century. The tale describes the funeral of a poor man. "They cut through solid marble to make his grave and yet the little marble tombstone they put above him was from Vermont. They buried him in the heart of a pine forest, and yet his pine coffin came from Ohio. They buried him beside an iron mine, and yet the nails in his coffin and the iron in the shovel came from Pittsburgh. They buried him  in a coat from New York and shoes from Chicago and a shirt from Cincinnati. The South did not supply anything for the funeral except the body and the hole in the ground."

The point of the story was expressed by a modern southerner in this way: "We have added too little human skill to our raw material."

As this comment and the fable both suggest, geography itself has been kind to the Southeast. The region is blessed with plentiful rainfall and a mild climate. On most of its farmlands, crops can be grown without frost at least  six months of the year. A transportation artery, the Mississippi River and its southern branches, runs through the heart of the area, and other rivers are found near its coast. Crops grow easily in its soil, which is brown on the coastal plain, red on the low hillsides, and black in east Texas. The mountains contribute coal, water power, and rich valleys. Much of the Florida peninsula is a garden for **subtropical** fruits. Some of the nation's largest oil fields lie in the state of

Louisiana. The region is naturally rich in fisheries, forests and minerals.

And to delight the human sense of poetry and wonder, the Southeast has many landscapes of special beauty. For instance, there are low **water-covered** lands where cypress trees, shaped like **long-necked** wine bottles, rise out of dark, quiet waters into dark and tent-like masses of vines above. There is soil that looks like broad expanses of red silk, decorated with the long curving rows of pink and white flowers of the cotton plant. There are quiet little valleys hidden between great green hills, or sunny, sandy islands where all the world seems to be one endless stretch of sand, water, sky and wind.

Since the end of World War II, there has been a great **upturn** in the region's economic fortunes. Persons returning to the Southeast after many years' absence are astonished at the improvements they see: new roads, bridges and factories; new schools, hospitals and community centers.

The Southeast has needed these improvements badly. Even today the **average** income and the average standard of living of its people are lower than in any other region of the nation. Part of its natural population gain was lost because many people left to find greater opportunity in the North or West. The Southeast, as a whole, uses machine power less than other regions do, and the value of agricultural or industrial goods produced by each worker is less. Clearly, in this region, the **partnership** of man and geography did not develop as fully as elsewhere.

After You Read

Knowledge Focus

1. **Fill in the blanks according to the geographical knowledge you have learned in the text above.**
   (1) A transportation artery, _____ and its southern branches, runs through the heart of the Southeast.
   (2) In the Southeast of the USA, much of _____ is a garden for _____ fruits.
   (3) The state of _____ has some of the nation's largest oil fields.
   (4) On most of its farmlands, crops can be grown without frost at least _____ months of the year.
   (5) Since the end of World War _____, there has been a great upturn in the Southeast's _____ fortunes.
   (6) Today the average _____ and the average standard of living of the people in this region are _____ than in any other region of the nation.
   (7) The Southeast is blessed with plentiful rainfall and a mild _____.
   (8) There are altogether _____ states in the Southeast of USA.

2. Write T in the brackets if the statement is true and write F if it is false.

(1) The states of Kentucky, Tennessee, and Arkansas are located in the Southeast of the USA. ( )

(2) The Southeast does not have great rainfall because of the Appalachians. ( )

(3) It is rather cold in the Southeast, so crops can be grown without frost at best for four months. ( )

(4) The Southeast is naturally rich in fisheries, forests, and minerals. ( )

(5) The Southeast does not have any landscape of special beauty except the beaches. ( )

(6) People keep on leaving the Southeast for better opportunities. ( )

(7) People who come back to the Southeast after many years' absence are astonished at the downturn they see. ( )

(8) Florida is a peninsula rich in subtropical fruits. ( )

Language Focus

1. Fill in the blanks with the proper forms of the following expressions you have learned in the text.

be blessed with	lie in	cut through	be rich in
be decorated with	be astonished at	go back	be shaped like
add to	water-covered		

(1) People returning to the Southeast after many years' absence _____ the improvements they see.

(2) The story of a man's funeral _____ a decade before the turn of last century.

(3) Some of the nation's largest oil fields _____ the states in the Southeast of the USA.

(4) Geography itself has been kind to the Southeast, but the people have _____ too little human skill _____ our raw materials.

(5) The Southeast _____ much rainfall and a favorable climate.

(6) Cypress trees, _____ long-necked wine bottle, rise out of dark, quiet waters into dark, tent-like masses of vines above.

(7) They _____ solid marble to make his grave and yet the little marble tombstone they put above him was from Vermont.

(8) The region _____ naturally _____ _____ fisheries, forests and minerals.

(9) There is soil that looks like broad expanses of red silk, _____ _____ the long curving rows of pink and white flowers of the cotton plant.

(10) There are low _____ lands where cypress trees rise out of dark.

2. Fill in the blanks with the proper forms of the words in the brackets.

(1) The land of the southeastern region is old and _____ (exhaust), but it is being given a new life.

(2) The problems of the Southeast are best _____ (illustration) by a story of a man's funeral.
(3) A modern _____ (south) clearly expressed the point of the story in one sentence.
(4) The Southeast has _____ (plenty) rainfall and a mild climate.
(5) The Southeast has many landscapes of special _____ (beautiful).
(6) The soil looks like broad expanses of red silk, _____ (decoration) with the long _____ (curve) rows of pink and white flowers of the cotton plant.
(7) In the region of the Southeast, the _____ (partner) of man and geography did not develop as fully as elsewhere.
(8) There are _____ (sun) and _____ (sand) islands where the entire world seems to be one _____ (end) stretch of sand, water, sky and wind.
(9) Many people have returned to the region after years' _____ (absent).

3. **Fill in the blanks with the proper prepositions or adverbs that collocate with the neighboring words.**
   (1) The problems of the Southeast area are best illustrated by a story that goes _____ a decade before the turn _____ the last century.
   (2) They cut _____ solid marble to make his grave.
   (3) They buried him _____ the heart of a pine forest.
   (4) The South did not supply anything _____ the funeral _____ the body and the hole _____ the ground.
   (5) _____ most of its farmlands, crops can be grown _____ frost at least six months of the year in the Southeast of the USA.
   (6) Persons returning _____ the Southeast after many years' absence are astonished _____ the improvements they see.
   (7) Even today the average income and the average standard _____ living of its people are lower than _____ any other region of the nation.
   (8) The Southeast, _____ a whole, uses machine power less than other regions do.

4. **Fill in the blanks with the comparative degree of adjectives or adverbs according to Text A.**
   (1) The southeastern region is changing _____ than any other part of the US.
   (2) Even today the average income and the average standard of living of its people _____ than in any other region of the nation.
   (3) Part of its natural population gain was lost because many people left to find _____ opportunity in the North or West.
   (4) The Southeast, as a whole, uses machine power _____ than other regions do.
   (5) The value of agricultural and industrial goods produced by each worker in the Southeast is _____ than in other regions.

Comprehensive Work
1. **Pair Work**: Locate and label the southeastern states on the outline map below with your

partner.

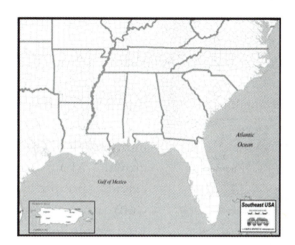

2. Group Work: Discuss the following questions in groups of three or four members according to the geographical knowledge you have already acquired. You can make use of certain maps of the USA, take some notes, if necessary, and present the view points of your group to the class. **Note:** You are encouraged to make use of the Internet resources for this purpose after class.
(1) What problem has the Southeast encountered? What favorable conditions does it enjoy? And what progress has it witnessed in recent years?
(2) What are the similarities and differences between the Northeast and the Southeast of the USA?

3. Solo Work: Write a composition, comparing and contrasting the Chinese southeastern region with that of the United States in terms of geography.

Read the passage quickly and try to find the information to fill in the following blanks.
(1) Miami is located in the state of _____. Its spectacular population growth is due to migration from _____.
(2) New Orleans is located in the state of _____.
(3) Orlando, located in _____, has grown explosively as a _____ and _____ center.
(4) Jacksonville, Tampa, and Fort Lauderdale in the state of _____ have swelled from migration of _____ from northern states.

The population of Florida has grown **spectacularly**. Florida's population in 2008 was 18,089,888, more than 18 times the size of its 1920 population of 968,470.

Major cities in the region include Miami, Florida and New Orleans, Louisiana. Urban areas, especially the larger ones, are significant destinations for migrants, particularly by people from outside the region.

The cities of Florida have **absorbed** most of the state's rapid population growth. Miami has grown, to a large extent, because of migration from Cuba after a communist government was established in Cuba in the early 1960s. Orlando has grown **explosively** as a convention and tourist center. Jacksonville, Tampa, and Fort Lauderdale have **swelled** from migration of retirees from northern states. Smaller Florida cities such as Destin, a weekend resort location, and West Palm Beach, a winter resort and tourist heaven, have also experienced **stunning** growth.

Text C   The Top in the Southeast

Read the following passage and find out *the oldest*, *the first*, and *the most* about the Southeast of the USA.

The oldest permanent European settlement is St. Augustine, Florida. The Spanish founded it in 1565.

The first English colony in the Americas was on Roanoke Island in Virginia. It was founded in 1583 by Sir Walter Raleigh. But its settlers disappeared. No one knows what happened to them.

In 1700s, Charleston, South Carolina, was the wealthiest city in the South. It had the first public library, the first theatre, and the first museum in the colonies.

More Presidents of the USA were born in Virginia than in any other state. The total is eight so far: George Washington (first), Thomas Jefferson (third), James Madison (fourth), James Monroe (fifth), William Henry Harrison (ninth), John Tyler (tenth), Zachary Taylor (twelfth), and Woodrow Wilson (twenty-eighth).

Unit 6　Land of Changes in the Southeast

Proper Names

Arkansas 阿肯色州
Charleston 查尔斯顿（南卡罗来纳州一城市）
Chicago 芝加哥（美国第三大城市，位于伊利诺伊州）
Cincinnati 辛辛那提（俄亥俄州西南部一城市）
Cuba 古巴
Destin 达斯汀城（佛罗里达州一城市，被誉为"世界上最幸运的渔村"）
Florida 佛罗里达州
Fort Lauderdale 劳德代尔堡（佛罗里达州一城市，被誉为"美国的威尼斯"）
George Washington 乔治·华盛顿（美国第一任总统）
Henry Ford 亨利·福特（美国汽车工程师和企业家，福特汽车公司的建立者）
Houston 休斯敦（美国第四大城市，位于得克萨斯州）
Jacksonville 杰克逊维尔（佛罗里达州第一大城市）
James Madison 詹姆斯·麦迪逊（美国第四任总统）
James Monroe 詹姆斯·门罗（美国第五任总统）
John Tyler 约翰·泰勒（美国第十任总统）
Kentucky 肯塔基州

Louisiana 路易斯安那州
Latin America 拉丁美洲
Miami 迈阿密（佛罗里达州东南部一著名城市）
Mississippi 密西西比州
Mobile 莫比尔（阿拉巴马州南部一城市）
New Orleans 新奥尔良市（美国主要港市之一，路易斯安那州第一大城市）
North Carolina 北卡罗来纳州
Ohio 俄亥俄州
Orlando 奥兰多市（佛罗里达州中部一主要城市）
Pensacola 潘沙克拉（佛罗里达州一城市）
Roanoke Island 罗厄诺克岛（北卡罗来纳州沿海岛屿）
Sir Walter Raleigh 沃尔特·罗利爵士
South Carolina 南卡罗来纳州
St. Augustine 圣奥古斯丁（佛罗里达州一古老港口）
the Atlantic Coast 大西洋海岸
the Continental Shelf 大陆架
the Gulf of Mexico 墨西哥湾
the Intracoastal Waterway（美国大西洋沿岸）近岸内航道

Tampa 坦帕市(佛罗里达州西海岸一城市)
Tennessee 田纳西州
Texas 得克萨斯州
Thomas Jefferson 托马斯·杰斐逊(美国第三任总统)
West Palm Beach 西棕榈滩(佛罗里达州一城市)
West Virginia 西弗吉尼亚州
William Henry Harrison 威廉·亨利·哈里森(美国第九任总统)
Woodrow Wilson 伍德罗·威尔逊(美国第二十八任总统)
Zachary Taylor 扎卡里·泰勒(美国第十二任总统)

For Fun

Websites to visit

http://archaeology.about.com/od/americansoutheast/American_Southeast_Culture_History_and_Archaeology.htm

This is a webpage about the culture history, archaeological sites, and other information related to the past of the southeastern United States.

Movies to see

Sweet Home Alabama

Melanie (Reese Witherspoon) is happily living in New York, with her boyfriend. When he proposes to her, she accepts and has to return home, to Alabama, to rid herself of another husband she has been hiding, by having a different name. Jake, the husband, refuses to sign divorce papers throughout the movie, making Melanie stay in Alabama (determined to get him to sign them) and rediscover who she is.

Vernon, Florida

It is an odd-ball survey of the inhabitants of a remote swamp-town in the Florida panhandle. Henry Shipes, Albert Bitterling, Roscoe Collins and others discuss turkey-hunting, gator-grunting and the meaning of life. This second effort by Errol Morris, originally titled "Nub City," was about the inhabitants of a small Florida town who lop off their limbs for insurance money ("They literally became a fraction of themselves to become whole financially," Morris commented.) but had to be retooled when his subjects threatened to murder him. Forced to come up with a new concept, Morris created "Vernon, Florida" (1981) about the eccentric residents of a Southern swamp town.

Songs to enjoy

"Give Me Louisiana"
Written by Doralice Fontane
Composed by John Croom

Give me Louisiana,
The state where I was born
The state of snowy cotton,
The best I've ever known;
A state of sweet magnolias,
And Creole melodies.
Oh give me Louisiana,
The state where I was born
Oh what sweet old memories
The mossy old oaks bring.
It brings us the story
Of our Evangeline.
A state of old tradition,
of old plantation days
Makes good old Louisiana
The sweetest of all states.

Give me Louisiana,
A state prepared to share
That good old southern custom,
Hospitality so rare;
A state of fruit and flowers,
Of sunshine and spring showers.
Oh give me Louisiana,
The state where I was born

Its woodlands, its marshes
Where humble trappers live.
Its rivers, its valleys,
A place to always give.
A state where work is pleasure,
With blessings in full measure
Makes good old Louisiana
The dearest of all states.

Give me Louisiana,
Where love birds always sing
In shady lanes or pastures,
The cowbells softly ring;
The softness of the sunset
Brings peace and blissful rest.
Oh give me Louisiana,
The state where I was born
The smell of sweet clover
Which blossoms everywhere;
The fresh new mown hay
Where children romp and play.
A state of love and laughter,
A state for all here after
Makes good old Louisiana
The grandest of all states.

Unit 7
Touring the Southeast

> This country and its economy must have a vibrant commercial center at the mouth of the Mississippi River, its most important waterway...
>
> —Kathleen Blanco

Unit Goals

- To be familiar with the landform of the Southeast
- To have an idea of the famous spots in the Southeast
- To be familiar with the geographical terms about the Southeast
- To be able to describe the landform of the Southeast
- To be able to express cause and effect in different ways

Before You Read

1. Can you match the photos of the animals in the Southeast of the USA with their names? (raccoon, pony, bobcat, alligator)

2. What wetland is a great setting for a scary movie? Marshes at the Mississippi Delta? Not really! Try the Great Dismal Swamp, which is located in _____.

3. Match the wetlands with their features.

	filled with trees
marsh	with a few trees
	grassy
	with hanging vines
swamp	bright and sunny
	dark and mysterious

4. In the cartoon, the lady cannot rise to say "hello" because she is having a _____ at _____ in _____, a state located in the Southeast of the USA.

5. This is _____ _____, who is famous as _____ of _____. He was born in the state of Mississippi in 1935, and moved to the city of _____ in the state of _____ in 1948.

6. Form groups of three or four students. Try to find, on the Internet or in the library, more information about the tourist destinations in the Southeast of the USA which interests you. Prepare a 5-minute classroom presentation.

Start to Read

Text A   The Mighty Mississippi River and the Ozarks

The Mississippi is one of the world's greatest rivers. It runs 6,400 kilometers long. At the river's mouth, the fresh water of the river mixes with the salty water of the Gulf of Mexico. The river has brought lots of mud—about 13,000 square miles of it. About 400 million tons of mud is carried here every year from farmlands 2,000 miles away. That is how the watery landform called the Mississippi Delta gets its rich, dark soil.

Water in this delta region does not drain away. As a result, there are marshes **stretching** out in every direction. Only a few trees grow only where the ground is higher. Their shades of the trees are appealing, but sitting in the shade is dangerous. People can sink up to their waist in mud. Alligators just love these marshes. So do all the **wading** birds. With their long legs and long necks, they are able to wade in the water and find shrimp, crawfish, and other sorts of fish to eat. Under water, this quiet place is **teeming** with life.

Apart from the greatest river, there are the oldest mountains, the Appalachian Mountains. And besides the oldest mountains in the Southeast lies an area of beautiful mountains with natural springs where the water is really hot. That is the Ozark National Forest, one of the great wilderness areas of the Southeast. It is located in northwestern Arkansas in the Ozark Mountains. Visitors can stay in a log cabin in the woods and hike one of the many trails. The Ozarks also have many beautiful streams and lakes. In fact, one of the  most popular water activities here is floating—in canoes, kayaks, rafts, or johnboats. Johnboats are flat-bottomed boats used for fishing. There are lots of fish, such as trout and bass, if you want to try your luck.

In Arkansas, there are many natural hot springs—places where hot, clear spring water rises up out of the ground. The town of Hot Springs has 47 springs, **spouting** 3,028,000 liters of water every day. The water temperature can get as high as 63.9℃. That is hotter than our bath or shower.

Taking a trip up Hot Springs Mountain

to Hot Springs Tower is exciting. If you ride an elevator to the top of the tower, you can enjoy a view of the surrounding lakes, mountains, and valleys. On a clear day, you can see for 64 kilometers.

Text B Flat Plains and Islands

In the eastern part, the land gets flat. It is the **coastal plain**. This landform stretches from Virginia to Florida along the Atlantic and the Gulf coasts to Louisiana. In some areas, these plains are so flat that water hardly moves at all, resulting in wetlands like the Great Dismal Swamp in Virginia and North Carolina. These  wetlands are swamps, not marshes like the ones at the Mississippi Delta. The swamps are filled with trees and hanging vines. They are dark and **mysterious**. In the **dim** light under the trees and the tangle of vines, raccoons, bobcats, and even bears live, just like the great settings for a scary movie! They differ from the bright and sunny marsh in the Mississippi Delta because the lands are **grassy** with just a few trees.

The Southeast has hundreds of islands, too. Assateague Island off the Atlantic coast is favorite for many people.

Assateague Island is a sand dune, a long thin hill of sand. It is called a **barrier** island because it acts like a barrier, or wall, protecting the mainland from rough ocean waves. The island is famous for its wild ponies. Ponies have lived here for hundreds of years, wild and free.

Further south in the tropical waters off Florida is a special kind of island called a **key**. Keys are made from coral, limestone skeletons formed by tiny sea animals. Sometimes masses of coral get so big that they rise above the water, forming coral islands.

After You Read

Knowledge Focus

1. **Fill in the blanks according to the geographical knowledge you have learned in the texts above.**

    (1) The Mississippi River has brought lots of mud to its mouth, where the fresh water mixes with the salty water of _____, thus forming the watery landform called _____.

    (2) In the Southeast of the USA lies an area of beautiful mountains with natural _____ where the water is really hot. That is the Ozark National Forest, which is located in _____ in the Ozark Mountains.

    (3) On the _____ side of the Appalachian Mountains is the _____ Plateau. A plateau is an area of flat land that is _____ than the land round it.

    (4) The coastal plain in the Southeast stretches form Virginia to _____ along the Atlantic and the Gulf coasts to _____.

    (5) On the _____ side of the Appalachians is the _____ region, whose name is a French word, meaning _____.

    (6) The town of _____ has 47 springs, spouting 3,028,000 liters of water every day. The water temperature can get as high as _____ ℃.

    (7) A swamp and a marsh are different. While a _____ is grassy with just a few trees, a bright and sunny place, a _____ is filled with trees and hanging vines, a dark and mysterious place.

    (8) The Southeast has hundreds of islands, too. _____ Island off the Atlantic coast is many people's favorite. The island is famous for its wild _____.

    (9) Further south in the tropical waters off Florida, you will find a special kind of island called a _____, made from _____, limestone skeletons formed by tiny sea animals.

2. **Write T in the brackets if the statement is true, and write F if it is false.**

    (1) At the mouth of the Mississippi River, tourists can see lots of mud brought by the river. (   )

    (2) The wading birds can find a good variety of fish to eat in the marshes in the Mississippi Delta. (   )

    (3) The Ozark National Forest is located in Louisiana, where tourists can enjoy themselves in water activities and the hot springs. (   )

    (4) A plateau is an area of flat land that is lower than the land round it. (   )

    (5) The coastal plain is located in the southwest of the USA. (   )

    (6) A marsh is grassy with just a few trees in the dim light. (   )

    (7) A swamp is a dark place with many trees and hanging vines. (   )

    (8) Arkansas has many natural hot springs—places where hot, clear spring water rises up out of the ground. (   )

Language Focus

1. Fill in the blanks with the following expressions you have learned in the texts.

be teeming with	apart from	mix with	act like
be famous for	stretch out	as a result	drain away
up to	protect...from		

(1) Assateague Island _____ a barrier, or wall, _____ the mainland _____ rough ocean waves.

(2) At the mouth of the Mississippi River, the fresh water _____ the salty water.

(3) Under water, this quiet place _____ life.

(4) The water in the Mississippi Delta does not _____. So the wetlands _____ in every direction.

(5) A swamp looks dark _____ of overhead trees and vines.

(6) _____ the greatest river, there are the oldest mountains.

(7) Assateague Island _____ its wild ponies.

(8) People can sink _____ your waist in mud.

2. Fill in the blanks with the proper forms of the words in the brackets.

(1) This landform is _____ (water) and _____ (grass).

(2) The _____ (mystery) area is full of _____ (hang) vines. What a great setting for a _____ (scare) movie!

(3) The Mississippi Delta is a favorite of all the _____ (wade) birds.

(4) In the Ozark Mountains, one of the most popular water activities here is _____ (float) in canoes, kayaks, rafts, or johnboats.

(5) Tourists can ride an _____ (elevate) to the top of the Hot Springs Tower for a view of the _____ (surround) lakes, mountains, and valleys.

(6) The Piedmont is a region of gently _____ (roll) hills at the foot of the mountains.

(7) The town of Hot Springs has 47 springs, _____ (spout) 3,028,000 liters of water every day.

(8) Here, the fresh water of the river mixes with the _____ (salt) water of the Gulf of Mexico.

3. Fill in the blanks with the proper prepositions and adverbs that collocate with the neighboring words.

(1) Wetlands, called marshes, stretch out _____ every direction!

(2) A few trees grow only where the ground is higher, but do not try to sit _____ their shade.

(3) The explorers sank up _____ their waists in mud.

(4) Johnboats are flat-bottomed boats used _____ fishing.

(5) You can ride an elevator _____ the top of the tower _____ a view of the surrounding lakes, mountains, and valleys.

(6) _____ a clear day, you can see _____ 64 kilometers.

(7) If you look at the map, you will see that this landform stretches from Virginia to Florida _____ the Atlantic and the Gulf coasts to Louisiana.

(8) _____ the dim light under the trees and the tangle of vines, raccoons, bobcats, and even bears live.

4. Analyze the following sentences and discuss with your partner the different ways in which cause and effect is expressed. And rewrite the sentences in alternative ways.

(1) In some areas, these plains are so flat that water hardly moves at all, resulting in wetlands like the Great Dismal Swamp.

(2) Sometimes masses of coral get so big that they rise above the water, forming coral islands.

(3) About 400 million tons of mud is carried here every year from farmlands 2,000 miles away. That is how the watery landform called the Mississippi Delta gets its rich, dark soil.

(4) Water in this delta region does not drain away. As a result, there are marshes stretching out in every direction.

(5) With their long legs and long necks, the wading birds are able to wade in the water and find shrimp, crawfish, and other sorts of fish to eat.

(6) They differ from the bright and sunny marsh in the Mississippi Delta because the lands are grassy with just a few trees.

(7) It is called a barrier island because it acts like a barrier.

Comprehensive Work

1. Fill in the following table about the landforms in the Southeast.

Landform	Location	Features
Mississippi		
Ozarks		
Coastal Plains		
Great Dismal Swamp		
Assateague Island		
Keys		

2. Solo Work: Write a travel adventure story with 200 words about your trip through the Southeast America. Where will your adventure take place? What will happen? Plan your story below.

1. Where will my story take place? _____

_____

2. When will my story take place? _____
   _____
3. What characters will be in my story? _____
   _____
4. What problem will the characters have? How will they solve their problem?
   _____
   _____
   _____
5. How will the story end? _____
   _____

Read More

Text C   Memphis

Read the passage quickly and fill in the blanks with the information from the passage.

(1) Memphis is the _____ city in the state of _____. It sits on the banks of _____.
(2) Elvis Presley recorded his first two records at _____. _____ is his mansion. He is buried in _____.
(3) In Memphis, tourists cannot miss Mud Island, the National Civil Rights Museum and the _____, a sports and special events arena built to look just like the pyramids in Egypt.

Memphis is the largest city in Tennessee and it sits on the banks of the Mississippi River. The city is most famous for its music. It was the home of the "King of Rock and Roll," Elvis Presley. Elvis recorded his first two records in Memphis at Sun Studio, which is still there. Elvis's famous **mansion**, Graceland, is just outside of downtown Memphis and his **lavish** rooms, sparkling costumes, and gold records are still open to visitors. He was buried at Meditation Gardens.

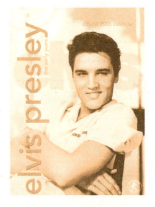

Mud Island is another tourist sight in the city. A monorail leads to this island park of 210,444 square meters. On the island, the Mississippi River Museum shows life on the river. Outside the museum is the River Walk, a five-block-long model of the Mississippi River.

The National Civil Rights Museum is also in this city. It is housed in the former Lorraine Motel, where Dr. Martin Luther King, Jr., was **assassinated** on April 4, 1968. The museum has exhibits about the important events and people of the civil rights movement.

Pyramid does not exist in Egypt only. The Pyramid in Memphis is a sports and special events arena built to look just like the pyramids in Egypt. Made of steel and glass, the Memphis Pyramid is one of the largest in the world, even taller than the Statue of Liberty!

Proper Names

Assateague Island 阿萨蒂格岛(马里兰州东南和弗吉尼亚州东部沿海的堤礁)
Dr. Martin Luther King, Jr. 小马丁·路德·金
Elvis Presley 埃尔维斯·普雷斯利(猫王)
Egypt 埃及
Graceland 雅园(猫王故居)
Hot Springs 温泉(镇)(阿肯色州一城市,因其天然温泉而得名)
Hot Springs Mountain 温泉山(阿肯色州)
Hot Springs Tower 温泉塔(阿肯色州)
Meditation Gardens 静默园/沉思园(猫王墓园)
Memphis 孟菲斯(田纳西州西南角一城市)
Mud Island 泥岛
Sun Studio 太阳录音室
the Great Dismal Swamp 北卡罗来纳州阴暗的大沼泽
the Memphis Pyramid 孟菲斯金字塔
the Mississippi Delta 密西西比三角洲
the Mississippi River Museum 密西西比河博物馆
the National Civil Rights Museum 国家人权博物馆
the Ozark Mountains 欧扎克山
the Ozark National Forest 欧扎克国家森林

For Fun

Websites to visit

http://blog.sina.com.cn/s/blog_4cbb496b0100088z.html

　　This is a Chinese blog page about the Mississippi River.

http://www.elvis.com/

　　This is the official website of the King of Rock 'n' Roll—Elvis Presley, on which you can find all kinds of information about him and his great music.

http://www.state.ar.us/

　　This is the official site for the state of Arkansas, on which you can find information about Arkansas's government, business, education, travel, etc.

Works to Read

Dred, a Tale of Great Dismal Swamp 1856

　　It is the second novel from American author Harriet Beecher Stowe. It was first published in two volumes by Phillips, Sampson and Company in 1856. Although it enjoyed better initial sales than her previous, and more famous, novel *Uncle Tom's Cabin*, it was ultimately less popular. *Dred* was of a more documentary nature than *Uncle Tom's Cabin* and thus lacked a character like Uncle Tom to evoke strong emotion from readers.

Movies to see

Jailhouse Rock

　　Vince Everett is serving a one-year jail sentence for manslaughter. While in the big house, his cellmate, a former country singer, introduces him to the record business. Everett takes to it so well that he decides to become a singer when he gets out. However, he is quickly disillusioned by the record business. But with the help of a new friend, he decides to form his own label, and soon becomes an overnight sensation. But when he becomes a superstar, will his desire for fame and money cause him to forget the people who got him there?

Songs to enjoy

"Ol' Man River" by Paul Robeson

　　"Ol' Man River" (music by Jerome Kern, lyrics by Oscar Hammerstein II) is a song in the 1927 musical *Show Boat* that tells a melancholy story of African American hardship and struggles of the time, related to the endless flow of the Mississippi River, from the view of a dock worker on a showboat.

There is an old man called Mississippi,
That's the old man I don't like to be.
What does he care if the world' d got troubles,
What does he care if the land ain' t free.

Don't look up, and don' t look down!
You don't just make the white boss frown.
Bend your knees and bow your head,
And pull that rope until you're dead!

Let me go way from the Mississippi,
Let me go way from the white man boss.
Show me that stream called de river Jordan,
Dat's de old stream dat I long to cross.

Old man river,
Dat old man river!
He must know something,
But don't say nothing.

He just keeps rolling,
He keeps on rolling along.

He don't plant tatoes,
He don't plant cotton,
And dem dat plant'em
Is soon forgotten,
But old man river,
He just keeps rolling along.

You and me we sweat and strain,
Body all aching and racked with pain.
Tote dat barge and lift dat bale,
Get a little drunk and you land in jail.

But I keep laughing instead of crying,
I must keep fighting until I'm dying,
But old man river,
He just keeps rolling along.

Unit 8

View of the Midwest

> There are extraordinary similarities between the Midwest in America and Europe in that there is this sense of vast, open sky and loneliness and cold.
>
> —Ajay Naidu

Unit Goals

- To have a general idea of physical features of the Midwest
- To be familiar with the landform of the Midwest
- To grasp the geographical terms about the landform of the Midwest
- To be able to describe the tourist attractions in the Midwest
- To be able to explain how the lakes, plains, badlands in the Midwest were formed
- To have a better understanding of noun clauses

Before You Read

1. The Great Lakes are the largest group of _____ lakes in the world. They were formed by _____. There are _____ Great Lakes in all. From largest to smallest they are Lake _____, Lake Huron, Lake Michigan, Lake Erie, and Lake _____.
2. Have you ever heard of the Badlands National Park? It is a special landform in the Midwest. Circle the adjectives that can be used to describe the land there.

   fertile   barren   rich   productive
   sterile   abundant   arid   fruitful
3. Sleeping Bear Dunes National Park is located by Lake _____. It got its name because once one really big dune was shaped like _____.
4. Do you know the following basketball teams in the Midwest of the USA? Where are their homes?

5. Form groups of three or four students. Try to find, on the Internet or in the library, more information about the tourist destinations in the Midwest of the USA which interests you. Prepare a 5-minute classroom presentation.

Start to Read

Text A Physical Features of the Midwest

The Midwest (the Midwestern United States, also referred to the Heartland) consists of twelve states: Illinois, Indiana, Iowa, Kansas, Michigan, Minnesota, Missouri, Nebraska, North Dakota, Ohio, South Dakota, and Wisconsin.

While it is true that these states are relatively flat, there is yet a measure of geographical variation. In particular, the eastern Midwest, lying near the foothills of the Appalachians, and the Great Lakes Basin demonstrate a high degree of topographical variety. Prairies cover most of the states west of the Mississippi River with the exception of central Minnesota and the Ozark Mountains of southern Missouri. Illinois lies within an area called the "prairie peninsula," an eastward extension of prairies that borders **deciduous** forests to the north, east, and south. Rainfall decreases from east to west, resulting in different types of prairies, with the tallgrass prairie in the wetter eastern region, mixed-grass prairie in the central Great Plains, and shortgrass prairie towards the rain shadow of the Rockies. Today, these three prairie types largely correspond to the corn/soybean area, the wheat belt, and the western rangelands, respectively. Although hardwood forests in the northern Midwest were logged to extinction in the late 1800s, they were replaced by new growth. The majority of the Midwest can now be categorized as urbanized areas and pastoral agricultural areas.

Text B　　Landform of the Midwest

Lakes Great and Small

We will begin our travels in Minnesota. We can see lakes everywhere. But it does not rain much here. Do you know where all this water came from? Think ice! About 18,000 years ago, all of Minnesota and most of the rest of the Midwest was covered with ice almost two miles thick! If you stood on top of that much ice, you would be about 10,000 feet above sea level!

A huge mass of ice like that is called a glacier. The glaciers were 10,000 feet thick and thousands of miles across. Imagine all that ice melting! All of these lakes are what is left of those glaciers.

The Great Lakes are the largest group of freshwater lakes in the world. They were once even bigger when the glaciers were melting. There are five Great Lakes in all. From the largest to the smallest they are Lake Superior, Lake Huron, Lake Michigan, Lake Erie, and Lake Ontario. The biggest one, Lake Superior, is the largest freshwater lake in the world.

A great place to visit is Sleeping Bear Dunes by Lake Michigan. The glaciers left enormous heaps of sand and gravel here. Long ago, one really big sand dune was shaped like a sleeping bear! That's how the park got its name.

Flat Plains and Big Rivers

Today, most of the Midwest is flat. But the region was not always this flat. Can you guess what **scraped** and **squashed** it as flat as a pancake? The glaciers, of course! Glaciers **flattened** the hills and filled in the valleys. Farmers here thank those glaciers because flat land is easy to farm. The glaciers left behind lots of good soil, too.

Many big rivers flow through the Midwest. The Ohio River forms a boundary between the Midwest and the Southeast. It flows by the states of Ohio, Indiana, and Illinois. The Ohio River flows into even a bigger river, the Mississippi River. When a smaller river flows into a bigger river, it is called a **tributary**. The Ohio River is a tributary of the Mississippi River.

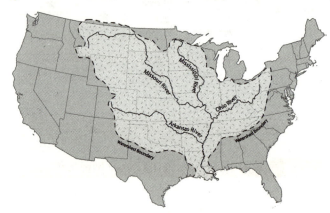

The biggest tributary of them all is the Missouri River. People around here call it the "Big Muddy." It is thick with mud—bits of rock carried all the way from the Rocky Mountains out west.

The Badlands

What do you think a place called the "badlands" might be like? We are now in South Dakota's big Badlands. The landforms here are sharp and jagged. Deep gullies, or long, narrow ditches, have been cut into the landscape. The badlands are very dry. You have to search  to find a plant or an animal here. The Native Americans and trappers of long ago named this area "badlands" because it was so hard to cross.

This area did not always look like this. Once, lots of animals lived here.

There were large cats with enormous fangs called **saber-toothed** cats. Camels lived here too, but they were about the size of dogs. Do you know how people know this? They have seen these animals' fossils. Fossils are the skeletons or **remains** of ancient plants and animals pressed into rock. You can find fossils of all kinds of plants and animals here.

The Caves

If you are going to visit Wind Cave, you will need to put on a jacket because it is always a nice cool 53℉ in here. Do not explore here alone. It is one of the bewildering "maze caves." It is easy to get lost in it. Over 90 miles of passageways have been explored in this cave.

When you explore the cave, hang on to your hats! The wind coming in and going out of the cave can reach 70 miles an hour! Do you know how to whistle? Wind Cave does. The wind going in and out of the mouth of the cave whistles!

If you like Wind Cave, you will like touring nearby Jewel Cave. It contains one of the longest cave systems (over 110 miles) in the United States. You will especially like the crystal jewels that decorate the cave's walls. It's the "jewels" that gave the cave its name.

After You Read

Knowledge Focus

1. **Fill in the blanks according to the geographical knowledge you have learned in the texts above.**
   (1) Among the Great Lakes, from the largest to the smallest they are Lake _____, Lake Huron, Lake Michigan, Lake Erie, and Lake _____.
   (2) _____ flattened the hills and filled in the valleys, thus making the Midwest as flat as a pancake.
   (3) The _____ River forms a boundary between the Midwest and the Southeast. It flows by the states of _____, Indiana and _____, and into a bigger river, _____.
   (4) The biggest tributary of the Mississippi is the _____, which is called the "Big Muddy," since it carries bits of rock all the way from the _____ Mountains out west.
   (5) The Native Americans and the trappers of long ago named the area in South Dakota "_____," because it was sharp and jagged, so hard to cross.
   (6) _____ is the flattest region in the United States with no mountain ranges.
   (7) _____ that decorate the cave's walls gave the cave its name—Jewel Cave.

(8) Fossils are the _____ or remains of ancient plants and _____ pressed into rock.

2. Write T in the brackets if the statement is true, and write F if it is false.
   (1) Farmers in the Midwest hate the glaciers because they flattened the land and made it difficult to farm. （　）
   (2) Generally speaking, the lakes in Minnesota, the Great Lakes and Sleeping Bear Dune National Park were all formed by the glaciers. （　）
   (3) There are not any animals or plants in the Badlands National Park. （　）
   (4) The Badlands were not always so dry. （　）
   (5) The Badlands are located in South Dakota. （　）
   (6) Wind Cave can make special sound. （　）
   (7) Visitors can see different jewels in Jewel Cave. （　）
   (8) All the states in the Midwest are very flat. （　）

3. Discuss the following questions with your partner.
   (1) Why are there so many lakes in Minnesota?
   (2) Where are the Ohio River and the Missouri River? And what different features do they have? Are they important?
   (3) Where are the Badlands in the USA? And why is the national park so named?

Language Focus
1. Fill in the blanks with the following words or expressions you have learned in the texts above.

scrape	hang on to	be shaped like	get lost
squash	put on	explore	look like
jag	decorate	heaps of	the rest of

   (1) _____ a jacket before you go into the cool Wind Cave, and _____ your hats when you are inside.
   (2) Wind Cave is like a maze, because over 90 miles of passageways have _____. Obviously, it is easy to _____ in it.
   (3) The glaciers left _____ sand and gravel here, among which, a sand dune _____ a bear, so the park got its name.
   (4) Most of the Midwest was not always flat. It was the glaciers then that _____ and _____ it as flat as a pancake!
   (5) The landforms in South Dakota are sharp and _____.
   (6) You will like the beautiful jewel-like rocks that _____ the cave's walls.
   (7) The Badlands did not always _____ this.
   (8) Long, long ago, all of Minnesota and most of _____ the Midwest was covered with ice.

2. **Fill in the blanks with the proper forms of the words in the brackets.**
    (1) You are totally wrong if you think the Midwest in the United States is _____ (mountain).
    (2) The Native Americans and the _____ (trap) long ago named this area in South Dakota "badlands" because it was so hard to cross.
    (3) There were large cats with enormous fangs called _____ (saber tooth) cats.
    (4) Fossils are the skeletons or _____ (remain) of ancient plants and animals _____ (pressure) into rock.
    (5) Wind Cave is one of the _____ (bewilder) "maze" caves.
    (6) The big sand dune was like a _____ (sleep) bear.
    (7) The glaciers _____ (flat) the hills and filled in the valleys.
    (8) The Missouri River is very _____ (mud).

3. **Fill in the blanks with the proper prepositions and adverbs that collocate with the neighboring words.**
    (1) Do you know where all the water come _____ ?
    (2) If you stood _____ top of that much ice, you would be about 10,000 feet _____ sea level!
    (3) A huge mass _____ ice like that is called a glacier.
    (4) Deep gullies have been cut _____ the landscape.
    (5) One really big sand dune was shaped _____ a sleeping bear!
    (6) The glaciers left _____ lots of good soil, too.
    (7) The Ohio River flows _____ the states of Ohio, Indiana, and Illinois.
    (8) The wind coming _____ and going _____ _____ the cave can reach 70 miles an hour!

4. **Read the following sentences and discuss with your partner what role the noun clauses play. And can you give examples of other roles that noun clauses play?**
    (1) It is true that these states are relatively flat.
    (2) Do you know where all this water came from?
    (3) All of these are what is left of those glaciers.
    (4) Can you guess what scraped and squashed it as flat as a pancake?
    (5) Do you know how people know this?
    (6) Into this area of industry came millions of Europeans who make of it what became known as the "melting pot."
    (7) What he cannot see is how the look of countryside has changed with this growth of industry.
    (8) It is where the President of the United States and about 250,000 government employees work.

Comprehensive Work
1. **Pair Work**: The following is the map of the Midwest of the USA. Talk about the location of the states with your partner, write their full names, and locate the rivers,

lakes and other well-known geographical spots in this region.

2. Solo Work: Writing—A Travel Article

You are to write an article for the travel section of a newspaper about a place in the Midwest America. Your article is expected to describe the place and explain why it makes a great travel destination. To help you choose a place to write about, answer these questions.

(1) Which place or attraction in the Midwest would I like to visit?
_____

(2) After you decide on a destination to write about, use this checklist to make sure you include all the important information people will want to know about that place.

★ Opening sentence to convince people to read your article: _____

★ The location: _____
★ Three phrases that describe the place: _____
_____
_____
_____

★ Importance of the place:
Geographically _____
Economically _____
Culturally _____
★ Three reasons people should visit: _____
_____
_____

★ Closing sentence to sum up your ideas: _____
_____
_____

Text C   Mount Rushmore National Memorial

Read the passage quickly and write T in the brackets if the statement is true, and write F if it is false.

(1) Mount Rushmore was created by Charles E. Rushmore. (   )
(2) The words by the sculptor in the second paragraph suggest that he was worried about his work's endurability. (   )
(3) The mountain was very suitable for the sculptor because of its height, its soft grainy granite and the length of time it catches the sun everyday. (   )
(4) The four presidents carved are George Washington, Thomas Jefferson, Abraham Lincoln and Theodore Roosevelt. (   )
(5) The carving begun in 1927 and ended in 1941. (   )
(6) Mount Rushmore is located in the Black Hills of South Dakota. (   )
(7) By 1998, a lot of facilities had been added to the Memorial. (   )
(8) The word "subdue" in the last paragraph probably means overcome. (   )

　　Mount Rushmore National Memorial, located 23 miles southwest of Rapid City, is something you do not want to miss. It is the greatest free attraction in the US!

　　"Until the wind and the rain alone shall wear them away." Those are the famous words Sculptor Gutzon Borglum used to describe the length of time his most famous work, Mt. Rushmore, will endure.

　　The mountain itself was **originally** named after Charles E. Rushmore, a New York lawyer investigating mining claims in the Black Hills in 1885. Gutzon Borglum chose this mountain due to its height (5,700 inches above sea level), the soft grainy consistency of the granite, and the fact that it catches the sun for the greatest part of the day. The presidents were selected on the basis of what each symbolized. George Washington① represents the struggle for independence, Thomas Jefferson② the idea of government by the people, Abraham Lincoln④ for his ideas on equality and the permanent union of the states, and Theodore Roosevelt③ for the 20th century role of the United States in world affairs. The carving of Mt. Rushmore actually began on August 10, 1927, and spanned a length of 14 years. Only about six and a half years were spent actually carving the mountain, with the rest of the time being spent on weather delays and Borglum's greatest enemy—the lack of funding. The total cost of the project was $900,000. Work continued on the project until the death of Gutzon Borglum in 1941. No carving has been done on the mountain since that time and none is planned in the future.

The granite faces of four American presidents' are scaled to men who would stand 465 feet tall! (George Washington's carved face is taller than a five-story building.) President Calvin Coolidge believed Mount Rushmore was "decidedly American in its conception, magnitude and meaning. It is altogether worthy of our country," Coolidge proclaimed at the dedication of the project in 1927.

The most spectacular program at Mount Rushmore is the evening lighting ceremony held in the new amphitheater, 9:00 P.M. sharp, a must-see when you are touring the beautiful Black Hills of South Dakota.

A $56 million redevelopment was completed in 1998 with the addition of a new parking structure, amphitheater, museum/theater complex, Visitor Orientation Center, Presidential Trail, gift shop, bookstore, and dining facilities. To complete your Rushmore experience, view the evening lighting ceremony. The National Park Service sponsors a special program

Memorial Day through Labor Day. It consists of a 10-minute talk followed by a 20-minute film. The highlight of the evening is the slow exposure of light to the monument until it is fully **illuminated**. It is a good idea to go early and bring a jacket. Program times are as follows: 9:00 – 9:30 P.M. lighting ceremony, 9:30 – 10:30 P.M. illumination. For these traveling in the off season, the faces are illuminated **nightly**. There are few people who are not **subdued** by the moments as they gaze upon the beauty of Mt. Rushmore. Just as the monument challenged its creator, so should its **splendor** challenge its viewer.

Proper Names

Abraham Lincoln 亚伯拉罕·林肯(美国第十六任总统)
Ajay Naidu 埃加利·奈杜
Calvin Coolidge 卡尔文·柯立芝(美国第三十任总统)
Charles E. Rushmore 查尔斯·E.拉什莫尔(美国著名律师)
George Washington 乔治·华盛顿(美国第一任总统)
Gutzon Borglum 格曾·博格勒姆(美国艺术家、雕刻家)
Illinois 伊利诺伊州
Indiana 印第安纳州
Iowa 依阿华州
Jewel Cave 宝石洞穴
Kansas 堪萨斯州
Lake Erie 伊利湖
Lake Huron 休伦湖
Lake Michigan 密歇根湖
Lake Ontario 安大略湖
Lake Superior 苏必利尔湖
Michigan 密歇根州
Minnesota 明尼苏达州
Missouri 密苏里州
Mount Rushmore National Memorial 拉什莫尔山国家纪念公园
Native Americans 北美土著
Nebraska 内布拉斯加州
North Dakota 北达科他州
Ohio 俄亥俄州
Presidential Trail 总统之路
Rapid City 拉皮德城(南达科他州第二大城市)
Sleeping Bear Dunes National Park 睡熊滩国家公园
South Dakota 南达科他州
the Badlands National Park 恶地(国家公园)
the "Big Muddy" 大泥河(密苏里河昵称)
the Black Hills 布拉克山(又译"黑山""黑丘",主要位于南达科他州)
the Central Great Plains 中央大平原
the Driftless Area 无碛带(美国中西部)
the Great Lakes Basin 五大湖盆地
the Heartland 中心地带
the Midwest 美国中西部
the National Park Service 国家公园管理局
the Ohio River 俄亥俄河
the Rockies 落基山脉
Theodore Roosevelt 西奥多·罗斯福(美国第二十六任总统)
Visitor Orientation Center 游客服务中心
Wind Cave 风穴(国家公园)
Wisconsin 威斯康辛州

For Fun

Websites to visit
http://www.badlands.national-park.com/
   This site is dedicated to providing useful information on Badlands National Park. You can learn about the park's history and wildlife, and discover scenic hiking trails and beautiful campgrounds.

http://www.wind.cave.national-park.com/
   This site is dedicated to providing useful information on Wind Cave National Park. You can learn about the park's history and wildlife, discover scenic hiking trails and beautiful campgrounds.

http://www.nps.gov/jeca/
   This is a page about Jewel Cave National Monument, on which you can find information on its history, culture, photos, etc.

Works to read
Winesburg, Ohio

   A critically acclaimed work of fiction by the American author Sherwood Anderson, the book, published in 1919, is a collection of related short stories, which could be loosely defined as a novel. The stories are centered on the protagonist George Willard and the fictional inhabitants of the town of Winesburg, Ohio.

Movies to see
Badlands (1973)

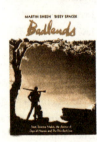

   It is a dramatization of the Starkweather-Fugate killing spree of the 1950's, in which a teenage girl and her twenty-something boyfriend slaughtered her entire family and several others in the Dakota badlands.

Songs to enjoy
"**Badlands**" by Bruce Springsteen

Lights out tonight, trouble in the heartland.
Got a head-on collision, smashin' in my guts man.
I'm caught in a crossfire that I don't understand.
But there's one thing I know for sure girl:
I don't give a damn for the same old played out scenes
I don't give a damn for just the in-betweens.
Honey I want the heart, I want the soul, I want control right now.
You better listen to me baby:
Talk about a dream; try to make it real.
You wake up in the night with a fear so real.
You spend your life waiting for a moment that just don't come.
Well don't waste your time waiting.

Badlands you gotta live it every day
Let the broken hearts stand
As the price you've gotta pay
We'll keep pushin' till it's understood
And these badlands start treating us good

Workin' in the field till you get your back burned
Workin' 'neath the wheels till you get your facts learned.
Baby I got my facts learned real good right now.
You better get it straight darling:
Poor men wanna be rich, rich men wanna be kings,
And a king ain't satisfied till he rules everything.
I wanna go out tonight, I wanna find out what I got.
Now I believe in the love that you gave me.
I believe in the faith that could save me.
I believe in the hope and I pray that some day it
Will raise me above these
Badlands...

For the ones who had a notion, a notion deep inside
That it ain't no sin to be glad you're alive.
I wanna find one face that ain't looking through me
I wanna find one place, I wanna spit in the face of these
Badlands...

Unit 9
More about the Midwest

> Water has an endless horizon; there is no limitation when you look out into the water. There's nothing to interfere with the mind's eye projecting itself as far as it can possibly imagine. I suppose it's the same way people in the Midwest feel about watching amber waves of grain or endless rows of cornfields. There is something exhilarating about it.
>
> —Billy Joel

Unit Goals

- To have a general idea about the pioneers' settlement in the Midwest
- to be able to describe how the adventurous families experimented with the prairie sod
- To be familiar with the past and the present of the Midwest
- To be able to give a brief introduction to Chicago
- To be able to use the non-restrictive clauses more skillfully

Before You Read

1. Here are some verbs and nouns about the settlement in the Midwest. Can you match them up? Remember that some words can match more than one word.

chop	a barn
clear	a tree
build	the forest
plant	a farm
expand	corn
sell	agriculture

2. Mark 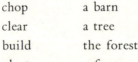_____, an American author and humorist,

grew up in Hannibal, Missouri on the _____ River.
3. Michael _____ joined the NBA's _____ Bulls, and later his leaping ability earned him the nicknames "Air Jordan" and "His Airness." This city is the _____ city in the Midwest and the _____ largest city in the nation.
4. Form groups of three or four students. Try to find, on the Internet or in the library, more information on the Midwest of the USA, such as its economy, agriculture or its largest city—Chicago, which interests you. Prepare a 5-minute classroom presentation.

Start to Read

Text A   Settlement on the Plains

For almost the first 200 years of American settlement, the only way to make a new farm was by **clearing** the forest, which was a long, hard job. Many of the trees were giants, so big that a man might **chop** for two days before he could **fell** one. The pioneer farmer also had to build his house and barn, his fences and often his own furniture and tools. At best, he could hope to clear only about one hectare each year. Because the stumps of the trees would **resist** burning or **loosening**, the farmer plowed and planted corn around and between them. Hidden roots often broke his horse's **harness** or even the plow itself. But, after years of such effort—with a little more land cleared each season—a **good-sized** farm finally emerged among the tall trees. When new settlers arrived in great numbers, this cleared land became very valuable. The first frontier farmers, those with true pioneer **zeal**, would then sell the farm, buy better cattle and equipment, and move on again westward. In this way, the farmer's labor created capital for an **expanding** agriculture.

By the early 19th century, frontier farmers finally reached the edge of the great eastern forest. They had arrived at the eastern pocket of the prairie, in what is now the State of Illinois. Many of those who recorded their feelings told of their joy in leaving the dark forest and coming out into the sunny, open grasslands which rose and fell in low, **graceful** slopes.

The prairie soil was richer than most of the forest land. But the pioneers did not know this. In their experience and that of their fathers, the only good soil was soil in which trees grew. So they settled in the forest at the edge of the grass.

After some years, however, **latecomers** or unusually **adventurous** families decided to experiment with the open land. At first, they had serious problems. The wooden and cast-iron plows of the time could not cut through deep, thick prairie sod. New Englanders, with their experience in mechanics, invented a much larger, heavier plow which could break and turn the sod. But the soft soil **stuck** to the rough iron, making the plow so heavy that a team of six oxen could scarcely pull it. The solution to the problem was steel, which could be sharpened and **polished** smoothly. The first steel plow was made by a prairie farmer, using strips from an old saw, in 1833. A few years later, John Deere, one of the pioneer makers of farm machines in the United States, began to manufacture steel plows. Rapidly, the prairie became the nation's richest agricultural region.

Text B   The Past and Present of the Midwest

The Midwest is a cultural crossroads. Starting in the early 1800s, easterners moved there in search of better farmland, and soon Europeans bypassed the East Coast to migrate directly to the interior: Germans to eastern Missouri, Swedes and Norwegians to Wisconsin and Minnesota. The region's fertile soil made it possible for farmers to produce abundant harvests of cereal crops such as wheat, oats, and corn. The region was soon known as the nation's "breadbasket."

Most of the Midwest is flat. The Mississippi River has acted as a regional lifeline, moving settlers to new homes and foodstuffs to market. The river inspired two classic American books, both written by a native Missourian, Samuel Clemens, who took the pseudonym Mark Twain: *Life on the Mississippi* and *The Adventures of Huckleberry Finn*.

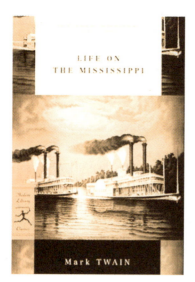
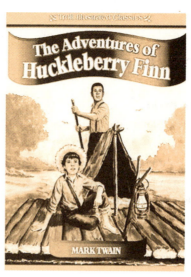

Midwesterners are praised as being open, friendly, and straightforward. Their politics tend to be **cautious**, but the **caution** is sometimes peppered with protest. The Midwest gave birth to one of America's two major political parties, the Republican Party, which was formed in the 1850s to oppose the spread of slavery into new states. At the turn of the century, the region also **spawned** the Progressive Movement, which largely consisted of farmers and merchants intent on making government less corrupt and more receptive to the will of the people. Perhaps because of their geographic location, many midwesterners have been strong adherents of **isolationism**, the belief that Americans should not concern themselves with foreign wars and problems.

The region's hub is Chicago, Illinois, the largest city in the region, followed by Detroit and Indianapolis. It is the nation's third largest city. This major Great Lakes port is a connecting point for rail lines and air traffic to **far-flung** parts of the nation and the world. At its heart stands the Sears Tower, at 447 meters, once the world's tallest building, which is named the Willis Tower now.

After You Read

Knowledge Focus

1. Fill in the blanks according to the geographical knowledge you have learned in the texts above.

(1) For almost the first 200 years of American settlement, the only way to make a new farm was by clearing _____.

(2) The first frontier farmers, those with true pioneer zeal, would then sell the farm, buy better cattle and equipment, and move on again _____.

(3) By the early 19th century, farmers finally reached _____ of the great eastern forest. They had arrived at the eastern pocket of the prairie, in what is now the State of _____.

(4) _____, with their experience in mechanics, invented a much larger, heavier plow which could break and turn the sod.

(5) Rapidly, the prairie became the nation's richest _____ region.

(6) The _____ is a cultural crossroads. Starting in the early 1800s, easterners moved there in search of better farmland, and soon _____ bypassed the _____ to migrate directly to the interior: _____ to eastern Missouri, _____ and _____ to Wisconsin and Minnesota.

(7) The _____ River has acted as a regional lifeline, moving settlers to new homes and foodstuffs to market.

(8) The region's hub is _____, Illinois, the nation's third largest city.

(9) At the heart of Great Lakes port stands the _____, at 447 meters, once the world's tallest building.

2. Write T in the brackets if the statement is true and write F if it is false.

(1) Because the stumps of the trees would resist burning or loosening, the farmer plowed and planted wheat around and between them. ( )

(2) The wooden and cast-iron plows of the time could not cut through deep, thick prairie sod. ( )

(3) Most of Midwest is flat. ( )

(4) The first steel plow was made by a prairie farmer, using strips from an old saw, in 1835. ( )

(5) The Midwest gave birth to one of America's two major political parties, the Democratic Party, which was formed in the 1850s to oppose the spread of slavery into new states. ( )

(6) Chicago is the nation's largest city. ( )

(7) Chicago is located in the state of Michigan. ( )

(8) Detroit is nicknamed the world's car capital. ( )

Language Focus

1. Fill in the blanks with the following words or expressions you have learned in the texts.

emerge	experiment with	manufacture
concern with	polish	stick to
consist of	sharpen	cut through
give birth to	inspire	

(1) She _____ herself _____ looking after the old people in her areas.
(2) The wooden and cast-iron plows could not _____ deep, thick prairie sod.
(3) After years of the effort, a good-sized farm _____ among the tall trees at last.
(4) Latecomers decided to _____ the open land.
(5) The city of New York _____ five boroughs.
(6) The new idea was for a steel plow to replace the wooden or cast-iron plow, which could be _____ and _____ smoothly.
(7) But the soft soil _____ the rough iron, making the plow so heavy that a team of six oxen could scarcely pull it.
(8) A few years later, John Deere, one of the pioneer makers of farm machines in the United States, began to _____ steel plows.
(9) The river _____ two classic American books, both written by a native Missourian, Mark Twain.
(10) The Midwest _____ one of America's two major political parties.

2. Fill in the blanks with the proper forms of the words in the brackets.

(1) When new settlers arrived in great numbers, the cleared land became very _____ (value).
(2) The first frontier farmers with true pioneer _____ (zealous), would then sell the farm, buy better cattle and _____ (equip), and move on again _____ (west).
(3) Many of those who recorded their _____ (feel) told of their joy in leaving the dark forest and coming out into the sunny, open grasslands which rose and fell in low, _____ (grace) slopes.
(4) After some years, latecomers or unusually _____ (adventure) families decided to do something with the open land.
(5) New Englanders came up with the _____ (solve) to the problem.
(6) Because the stumps of the trees would resist burning or _____ (loose), the farmer plowed and planted corn around and between them.
(7) But the soft soil stuck to the rough iron, making the plow so heavy that a team of six _____ (ox) could scarcely pull it.
(8) Their politics tend to be _____ (caution), but the caution is sometimes peppered with protest.
(9) Perhaps because of their geographic location, many Midwesterners have been strong _____ (adhere) of isolationism.
(10) This major Great Lakes port is a _____ (connect) point for rail lines and air

traffic to far-flung parts of the nation and the world.

3. Fill in the blanks with the proper prepositions and adverbs that collocate with the neighboring words.

(1) The only way was to make a new farm _____ clearing the forest.

(2) After years of such effort—_____ a little more land cleared each season—a good-sized farm finally emerged _____ the tall trees.

(3) They settled in the forest _____ the edge of the grass.

(4) They told _____ their joy _____ leaving the dark forest and coming out into the sunny, open grasslands which rose and fell _____ low, graceful slopes.

(5) The soft soil stuck _____ the rough iron.

(6) The first steel plow was made by a prairie farmer, using strips _____ an old saw, in 1833.

(7) The solution _____ the problem was steel, which could be sharpened and polished smoothly.

(8) _____ the turn of the century, the region also spawned the Progressive Movement, which largely consisted of farmers and merchants intent on making government less corrupt and more receptive _____ the will of the people.

(9) _____ its heart stands the Sears Tower, at 447 meters, the world's tallest building.

4. Translate the following sentences and discuss the roles of non-restrictive clauses in them with your partner.

(1) The only way to make a new farm was by clearing the forest, which was a long, hard job.

(2) The solution to the problem was steel, which could be sharpened and polished smoothly.

(3) The river inspired two classic books, both written by a native Missourian, Samuel Clemens, who took the pseudonym Mark Twain.

(4) The Midwest gave birth to one of America's two political parties, the Republican Party, which was formed in the 1850s to oppose the spread of slavery into new states.

(5) The region also spawned the Progressive Movement, which largely consisted of farmers and merchants intent on making government less corrupt and more receptive to the will of the people.

(6) Alaska, which is not included in the term "contiguous United States," is at the northwestern end of North America.

(7) In many towns there are old farmhouses and barns, which have been changed into dwellings, and now there are crowded close by taller buildings.

(8) Crops grow easily in its soil, which is brown on the coastal plain, red on the low hillsides, and black in east Texas.

Comprehensive Work

1. **Group Work:** Play an oral game in a group of three or four by using the states, cities and anything you are interested in the Midwest. A group member may start by saying: "I left Minnesota for Illinois because I want to visit Chicago—the largest city in the Midwest, with Zhang Hong (another group member's name)." Then Zhang Hong continues: "I left Illinois for Michigan because I want to visit Sleeping Bear Dunes, with..." No repetition of the state is permitted. And after your group finishes all the states there in the Midwest, you can start another round without repeating the cities or tourist attractions in the first round.

2. **Pair Work:** Discuss with your partner what differences there are between the Northeast and the Midwest of the United States in geography.

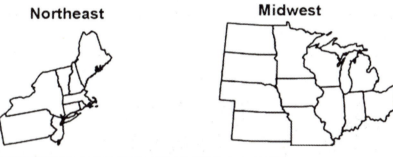

Category \ Region \ Difference	Northeast	Midwest

3. **Solo Work:** Write a poem or lyric about the pioneers' settlement in the forests and on the plains.

Read More

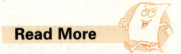

Text C   **Belts in the Midwest**

1. Locate the steel manufacturing centers on the map below.
2. Read the passage quickly and finish the following questions.
   (1) The Model T was made because Henry Ford wanted to make a good car affordable to _____.
   (2) _____ is one of the leading states in milk production.
   (3) Lots of the milk produced in the Midwest is made into _____, because cheese can _____.
   (4) The Corn Belt is also the Beef Belt and the Hog Belt because the extra _____ is eaten by _____ and _____.
   (5) The newly arrived farmers planted wheat on the ancient grasslands with few tree and turned the prairie into _____.

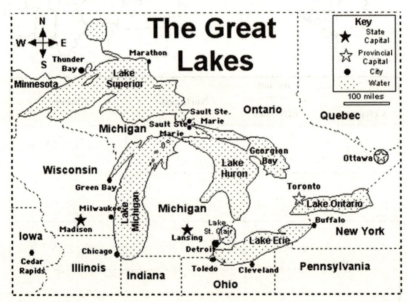

A Manufacturing Belt

For more than a hundred years Minnesota iron has been shipped to Chicago, the biggest transportation center in the country. In no other part of the country do railroad yards handle as much freight.

Coal from the Southeast is transported here by train. In Chicago's huge mills, iron and coal are used to make steel for bridges, cars, and skyscrapers.

Chicago is not the only place in the Midwest where steel is made. Shiploads of iron and trainloads of coal have made many Great Lakes cities into industrial giants. Cities like Milwaukee, Detroit, Toledo, and Cleveland are all manufacturing centers. They are all located in a wide row on the map, as if they were a belt.

If you like cars, please do not miss Detroit, the so-called "Motor City." Cadillacs, Lincolns, and Oldsmobiles are all made here. And the most famous car in history, the Model T Ford, was made in Detroit as well.

The Model T was more than just an ordinary car. It changed the Americans' life. Most early cars were handmade and were very costly. Only rich people could afford them. But young Henry Ford was determined to make a good car that working people could afford. In 1908, his first Model T cost $825, but it was still more than most people's annual income. Ford stuck to his dream. By 1915, he was selling car for $440 and by 1924, for $290. Ford's dream had come true.

The Dairy Belt

There are about 70 million kids under 18 years in the United States, and they are used to drinking two glasses of milk every day. That is thousands of tons of milk. Who can provide so much milk for American children?

The states in the Midwest.

Minnesota, Wisconsin, and Michigan have so many cows that the region is often called the Dairy Belt.

Take one of the states for example. Wisconsin is one of the leading states in milk production. There are over 1,300,000 cows. One cow may produce about 1,800 gallons of milk a year. 1,300,000 cows may produce more than people can consume.

Yes, Milk cannot be stored for very long, but cheese can. So lots of the milk produced in the Midwest is made into cheese. Wisconsin cheese is shipped to every state and to many other parts of the world.

The Corn Belt

Standing in the middle of an Iowa cornfield, you cannot see the end of the fields of green. Millions of them are grown from one end of this corn belt to the other.

How much corn do you think you eat a year? Think about corn on the cob, grits, cornbread, corn tortilla and tacos, corn chips, and then of course, popcorn. Most of Americans eat about 70 pounds of corn in one year. That is not enough to consume all of the corn grown in the Midwest.

Some corn is sent to countries around the world. But most of the extra corn is eaten by beef cattle and pigs. They just love it and eat lots of it, enjoying a life denied to many people in the underdeveloped countries. No wonder the Corn Belt is also the Beef Belt and Hog Belt!

The Wheat Belt

The Great Plains is in the Wheat Belt which stretches from North Dakota to Kansas. These rolling plains used to be vast grasslands with few trees. When settlers began to arrive on the prairie, no wheat grew here. But the newly arrived farmers planted wheat on the ancient grasslands. Soon, the region changed. The prairie was turned into wheat fields. Today, Midwesterners grow almost one billion bushels of wheat a year. That is enough to make breads and cereals for the Americans and still has enough left over to export to other countries.

Proper Names

Adventures of Huckleberry Finn 《哈克贝利·费恩历险记》
Cadillac 凯迪拉克(牌轿车)
Chicago 芝加哥(美国第三大城市,位于伊利诺伊州)
Cleveland 克利夫兰(俄亥俄州一城市)
Detroit 底特律(密歇根州第一大城市,美国中西部重要港市)
Henry Ford 亨利·福特(美国汽车工程师和企业家,福特汽车公司的建立者)
Indianapolis 印第安纳波利斯(印第安纳州首府)
Life on the Mississippi 《密西西比河上的生活》
Lincoln 林肯(牌轿车)
Mark Twain 马克·吐温
Milwaukee 密尔沃基(美国威斯康辛州东南部港市)
Motor City 汽车城(底特律的别称)
New Englanders 美国新英格兰居民
Norwegians 挪威人
Oldsmobile 奥兹莫比尔(牌轿车)
Samuel Clemens 塞缪尔·克莱门斯(美国小说家 Mark Twain 的真实姓名)
the Beef Belt 牛肉带(玉米带的别称)
the Corn Belt 玉米带
the Dairy Belt 奶制品带
the East Coast 东部沿海地区
the Great Plains 大平原
the Hog Belt 猪肉带(玉米带的别称)
the Model T Ford 福特 T 型车
the Progressive Movement 进步运动
the Republican Party 共和党
the Sears Tower 西尔斯塔
the Wheat Belt 小麦带
Toledo 托莱多(俄亥俄州一城市)

For Fun

Websites to visit

http://en.wikipedia.org/wiki/Great_Plains

    This is a webpage about the information on the Great Plains, including its geology, history, wind power, etc.

http://en.wikipedia.org/wiki/John_Deere

    This is a webpage about John Deere, an American blacksmith and manufacturer, who contributed a lot to the expansion of agriculture in the Midwest.

http://www.nationalgeographic.com/lewisandclark/

    This is a webpage on which you can read the information on Lewis and Clark's journey to explore the uncharted West.

Works to read
Lewis and Clark: A Prairie Dog for the President

Author Shirley Raye Redmond uses whimsy and humor to tell this historic event: President Jefferson sends the eager Lewis and Clark off to explore the West. The vast young nation has never been fully explored. The president wonders how long it will take to get to the end of it and what they will find.

Movies to see
Chicago

Murderesses Velma Kelly (a chanteuse and tease who killed her husband and sister after finding them in bed together) and Roxie Hart (Who killed her boyfriend when she discovered he was not going to make her a star) find themselves on death row together and fight for the fame that will keep them from the gallows in the 1920s Chicago.

Songs to enjoy
"Home on the Range"

"Home on the Range" is the state song of Kansas. Dr. Brewster M. Higley originally wrote the words in a poem called "My Western Home" in the early 1870s in Smith County, Kansas. The poem was first published in a December 1873 issue of the *Smith County Pioneer* under the title "Oh, Give Me a Home Where the Buffalo Roam." The music was written by a friend of Higley's named Daniel E. Kelley. Higley's original words are similar to those of the song today but not identical. The song was picked up by settlers, cowboys, and others and spread across the USA in various forms. In the early 20th century, it was arranged by Texas composer David Guion (1892—1981) who is often credited as the composer. It was officially adopted as the state song of Kansas on June 30, 1947, and is commonly regarded as the unofficial anthem of the American West.

Oh, give me a home, where the buffalo roam
And the deer and the antelope play
Where seldom is heard a discouraging word
And the skies are not cloudy all day.

Home, home on the range
Where the deer and the antelope play
Where seldom is heard a discouraging word
And the skies are not cloudy all day.

How often at night, when the heavens are bright

With the light from the glittering stars
I've stood there amazed, and asked, as I gazed
If their glory exceeds that of ours.

The air is so pure, and the zephyrs so free
And the breezes so balmy and light
I would not exchange my home on the range
For all the cities so bright.

The Red man was pressed from this part of the west
He's likely no more to return,

To the banks of the Red River where seldom if ever
Their flickering campfires burn.

Oh, I love these wild flowers in this dear land of ours
The curlew I love to hear cry
And I love the white rocks and the antelope flocks
That graze on the mountain slopes high.

Oh give me a land where the bright diamond sand
Flows leisurely down in the stream
Where the graceful white swan goes gliding along
Like a maid in a heavenly dream.

How often at night, when the heavens are bright
With the light from the glittering stars
Have I stood there amazed, and asked as I gaze
If their glory exceeds that of ours.

Yes, give me the gleam of a swift mountain stream
And the place no hurricanes blow
Oh, give me the park where the prairie dogs bark

And the mountains all covered with snow.

Oh, give me the hills and the ring of the drills
And the rich silver ore in the ground
Yes, give me the gulch where the miners can sluice
And the bright yellow gold can be found.

Oh, give me the mine where the prospectors find the gold in its own native land
And the hot springs below, where the sick people go
And camp on the banks of the Grand.

Oh, give me the steed and the gun that I need
To shoot game from my own cabin home
Then give me the camp where the fire is a lamp
And the wild rocky mountains to roam.

Yes, give me the home where the prospectors roam
Their business is always alive
In those wild western hills, midst the ring of the drills
Oh, let me live there 'till I die.

Unit 10
The Southwestern States

> Something called "the Oklahoma Standard" became known throughout the world. It means resilience in the face of adversity. It means a strength and compassion that will not be defeated.
> —Brad Henry

Unit Goals

- To have a general idea about the southwestern states
- To be familiar with the special features of the southwestern states
- To be able to tell the differences among the states in the Southwest
- To be able to use the infinitives more skillfully

Before You Read

1. Which four states are there in the Southwest of the USA? Locate and label them in the outline map.
2. The state of _____ in the Southwest is the second largest in the whole USA.
3. Do you know these basketball team logos? What teams do they symbolize respectively? Where are their homes?

4. Yao Ming, who was born in _____, People's Republic of China, is a professional basketball player who played for the _____ of the National Basketball Association. He was then the tallest player in the NBA, at 2.29m (7 feet 6 inches).

5. Match the state capitals with the states.

   Phoenix   Oklahoma
   Oklahoma City Texas
   Santa Fe   New Mexico
   Austin   Arizona

6. Form groups of three or four students. Try to find, on the Internet or in the library, more information on anyone of the Southwestern states in the USA which interests you. Prepare a 5-minute classroom presentation.

Start to Read

Text A Oklahoma & Texas

Oklahoma

Oklahoma is a land of flat, **fertile** plains and low hills. Oil and natural gas wells can be seen throughout much of the state. Oklahoma's plains also **host** large herds of cattle and vast wheat fields.

It is hard to imagine the **serene** fields and forests of today's Oklahoma as places of **frantic**, even **desperate** activity: Native American tribes forced to **relocate**; **land-crazed** settlers rushing to **claim** a piece of ground; Dust Bowl farmers escaping a state that was blowing away. Perhaps all that **agitation** made Oklahomans long for some quietness and relaxation, because that is what we find there today. Even the large cities of Tulsa and Oklahoma City seem uncrowded and unhurried, and Oklahomans everywhere in the state seem more than happy to engage visitors in some **leisurely** conversation.

The state has plenty of attractions for **tranquil** sightseeing, many of them related to the state's past, **turbulent** and otherwise. There are museums about cowboys, about cowboy philosophers (Will Rogers) and about the white settlers who moved into the area in the late 1800s and early 1900s. There are majestic tallgrass prairies that show the way the region looked before the cowboys and pioneers got there. Where Oklahoma really stands out, though, is **in its wealth of** Native American museums, historic sites and cultural gatherings. Once known as the Indian Territory, it still has the largest Native American population of any US state, numbering more than 500,000.

Texas

A drive across Texas has the **slippery**, **shifting** feel of a dream. Things change, and change significantly—from **bayous** and forests to prairies to **bare**, **windswept** plains. But the transformations are **subtle**. At some point, it will **dawn on** you that the trees have disappeared, but you will not be able to say exactly when.

Driving will likely be part of your visit to Texas. Unless you are planning to **confine** yourself to one place, you will be covering some territory—possibly a lot of territory—and you will likely be covering it in a car. The trick is to know how much is too much: Texas is a huge place. Unless you have got a lot of time (and a great fondness for road trips), you will want to set some limits and take the time to enjoy what you are seeing.

One of the state's big cities—Austin, Dallas, Fort Worth, Houston, and San Antonio—could **conceivably** fill a vacation by itself. But we suggest you combine one of them with visits to other less urban areas. The countryside offers so much variety—the wildflowers alone are worth a drive—and the huge blue sky is best appreciated from more-open spaces.

Text B New Mexico & Arizona

New Mexico

We can not **confirm** or **deny** the incident, but if aliens did crash their UFO in Roswell, they certainly picked the right state: New Mexico is **knee-deep** in

New Mexico

the **mystical** and the mysterious. Disappearing civilizations, secret atomic test sites, Native American healers, **divine** dirt and **miraculous** staircases are just some of the things you will find that are hard to explain.

The unknowable can be fun, but it is only a part of New Mexico's **allure**. Whether or not they hold powerful energy **vortexes**, the mountains and desert are beautiful to look at and thrilling to hike, bike, ski or raft through. Whether or not Pueblo people have the **remedy** for the ills of civilization, their art is engaging and their communities fascinating. We think you will have a completely enjoyable time taking New Mexico's scenery and activities **at face value**. If you happen to gain some spiritual **insight** (or meet an alien) along the way, so much the better.

Arizona

Though Arizona has become famous for its sunny skies and desert scenery, it is no **one-dimensional** state. In fact, on our last trip there, we ended up skidding through a December **blizzard** outside Flagstaff. We saw snow-covered pines rather than **towering** cacti.

Keep Arizona's **diversity** in mind when you plan your trip: There is more there than can be **absorbed** in one vacation. Our suggestion is to focus on a few areas that interest you—be it the popular **resort** areas (Phoenix, Scottsdale, Tucson or Sedona), natural wonders (the Grand Canyon or Saguaro National Park), Native American cultural sites (Canyon de Chelly or Navajo National Monument) or historic towns (Tombstone and Jerome). By **sampling** the state in small **helpings**, you will enjoy it more and leave plenty to explore the next time around.

After You Read

Knowledge Focus

1. Fill in the blanks according to the geographical knowledge you have learned in the text above.

(1) _____ is the state that has the largest Native American population of any US state, numbering more than 500,000.

(2) The white settlers moved into _____ in the late 1800s and the early 1900s, forcing the Native Americans to relocate.

(3) _____ is a large state, ranking the second largest state in the USA.

(4) _____ is the state, where you can find a lot that can be hard to explain, such as secret atomic test sites and Native American healers.

(5) Though _____ has become famous for its sunny skies and desert scenery, it is a state of diversity.

(6) Oklahoma is a land of flat, fertile _____ and low _____.

(7) Driving will likely be part of your visit to _____ in the Southwest, since it is so large.

(8) We cannot confirm or deny the UFO incident in Roswell, _____.

2. Write T in the brackets if the statement is true, and write F if it is false.

(1) Oklahoma has been always peaceful. ( )

(2) Oklahoma is in its wealth of Native American museums, historic sites and cultural gatherings. ( )

(3) Texas is huge, but such cities as Austin, Dallas, and Fort Worth in it are very small. ( )

(4) A drive across Texas has the feel of a dream, because it is so large that tourists feel very tired and sleepy when traveling in it. ( )

(5) New Mexico is skin-deep in the mystical and the mysterious. ( )

(6) New Mexico is located in the Southwest of the USA. ( )

(7) Arizona is no one-dimensional state. It is a state of diversity. ( )

(8) In Arizona, you can view desert, the Grand Canyon, historical towns and some Native American cultural sites. ( )

Language Focus

1. Fill in the blanks with the following words or expressions you have learned in the text.

confirm	long for	confine...to	end up
stand out	focus on	host	dawn on
claim	engage...in		

(1) Oklahomans _____ some quiet and relaxation after the turbulent past.

(2) Oklahomans feel quite happy to _____ visitors _____ some happy conversation.

(3) You have to cover some territory by car, if you do not want to _____ ourselves _____ one place in Texas.

(4) At some time, it will _____ you that something has changed in Texas, but you will not be able to say exactly when.

(5) Arizona is a state of variety, so our suggestion is to _____ a few areas that interest you.

(6) Where Oklahoma really _____, though, is in its wealth of Native American museums, historic sites and cultural gatherings.

(7) On our last trip there, we _____ skidding through a December blizzard.

(8) Land-crazed settlers rushed to Oklahoma to _____ a piece of ground.

(9) Oklahoma's plains _____ large herds of cattle and vast wheat fields.

(10) We cannot _____ the incident that the aliens crashed their UFO in New Mexico.

2. **Fill in the blanks with the proper forms of the words in the brackets.**

(1) Today's Oklahoma is a state of _____ (serene), but in the past, it was a place of _____ (desperate).

(2) Oklahomans would like to talk to visitors in a _____ (leisure) way.

(3) Oklahoma has plenty of sightseeing of _____ (tranquil).

(4) If you are not _____ (fondness) of road trips, just enjoy what you are seeing in Texas.

(5) In New Mexico, you would feel _____ (thrilling) to hike, bike or raft through the mountains, Pueblo people's communities have a great _____ (fascinating), and their art is _____ (engage).

(6) Arizona is not a one- _____ (dimension) state; it is a state with much _____ (diverse).

(7) Oklahomans became _____ (agitation) because of the frantic and desperate activity.

(8) Disappearing civilizations, _____ (mystery) Native American healers, _____ (divinity) dirt, and _____ (miracle) staircases would _____ (mystical) all the visitors.

(9) Oklahoma has a past of _____ (turbulent) or otherwise.

(10) It is _____ (conceivably) that one big city in Texas could fill your vacation itself.

3. **Fill in the blanks with the proper prepositions and adverbs that collocate with the neighboring words.**

(1) Oil and natural gas wells can be seen _____ much of Oklahoma.

(2) Dust Bowl farmers escaped a state that was blowing _____.

(3) Where Oklahoma really stands _____, though, is _____ its wealth of Native American museums, historic sites and cultural gatherings.

(4) Whether or not Pueblo people have the remedy _____ the ills of civilization, their art is engaging and their communities fascinating.

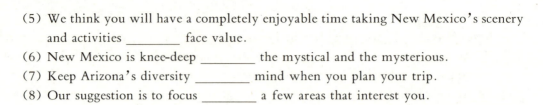

(5) We think you will have a completely enjoyable time taking New Mexico's scenery and activities _____ face value.
(6) New Mexico is knee-deep _____ the mystical and the mysterious.
(7) Keep Arizona's diversity _____ mind when you plan your trip.
(8) Our suggestion is to focus _____ a few areas that interest you.

4. **Discuss with your partner what the functions of the infinitives in the following sentences are.**

(1) It is hard to imagine the serene fields and forests of today's Oklahoma as places of frantic, even desperate activity.
(2) American tribes were forced to relocate.
(3) Unless you are planning to confine yourself to one place, you will be covering some territory in a car.
(4) The trick is to know how much is too much.
(5) Unless you have got a lot of time, you will want to set some limits and take the time to enjoy what you are seeing.
(6) If you happen to gain some spiritual insight along the way, so much the better.
(7) Our suggestion is to focus on a few areas that interest you.
(8) By sampling the state in small helpings, you will enjoy it and leave plenty to explore the next time around.

Comprehensive Work

1. **Pair Work:** Try to draw a picture of each state in the Southwest of the USA. Show and describe the pictures one by one to your partner and ask your partner to guess which state you are talking about.

2. **Group Work:** Associate one of the four states in the Southwest with one of your friends or classmates. Try to describe the characters or interests of this person, proving he would like to go there or he would not like to go there. And then form groups of three or four students to share your information with your group members.

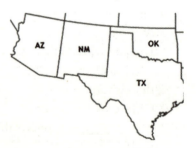

	Features	Characters/Habits/Interests	
State	_____	_____	
	_____	_____	
	_____	_____	Person
	_____	_____	

3. Solo Work: Which state do you prefer to visit of all the Southwestern states of the USA? Write a composition, giving at least three reasons for your preference.

Read More

Text C   Santa Fe, the City Different

Read the passage quickly and fill in the following blanks.
(1) The people of Santa Fe call their city _____.
(2) The city has many _____ buildings because of the lack of _____.
(3) The Palace of the Governors was built by the _____ almost 400 years ago.

The people of Santa Fe call their city "the city different." Many things in this city are unique. The city is different because of the many people who helped settle the area. Santa Fe has a rich and colorful history because it carries its Spanish, Mexican, and Native American heritage.

There are many adobe buildings in the city. Wood has never been used much for building because this region has few trees. Long ago, the Pueblo Indians mixed adobe clay with stones to build their apartment-style villages in this area. Later, the Spanish came and learned to use adobe bricks to set up buildings. In a region that is very hot in the summer and very cold in the winter, adobe buildings are warm in winter and cool in summer.

The Palace of the Governors is in Santa Fe. It was built by the Spanish almost 400 years ago. It is long and low, with thick walls built out of adobe. It does not look much like a palace, but many different governments have ruled here: first the Spanish, next the Native Americans, then the Mexicans, and finally the Americans. Today the Palace is the state history museum.

Proper Names

Austin 奥斯汀（得克萨斯州首府）
Arizona 亚利桑那州
Albuquerque 阿尔布开克（新墨西哥州第一大城市）
California 加利福尼亚州
Canyon de Chelly 谢伊峡谷
Colorado 科罗拉多州
Dallas 达拉斯（得克萨斯州第三大城市）
Flagstaff 费拉格斯塔夫（亚利桑那州北部一城市）
Fort Worth 沃斯堡（又译"福和市"，位于得克萨斯州北部）
Houston 休斯敦（美国第四大城市，位于得克萨斯州）
Jerome 杰罗姆（爱达荷州一城镇）
Las Trampas 拉特拉巴镇（新墨西哥州一城镇）
Navajo National Monument 那瓦霍国家纪念碑
New Mexico 新墨西哥州
Oklahoma 俄克拉何马州
Oklahoma City 俄克拉何马城（俄克拉何马州首府）
Oklahomans 俄克拉何马人
Phoenix 菲尼克斯（又译"凤凰城"，亚利桑那州首府及第一大城市）
Pueblo people 普韦布洛人（居住在新墨西哥北部与亚利桑那东北部的泥坯房里的北美土著人）
Roswell 罗斯威尔（新墨西哥州一城镇）
Scottsdale 斯考茨德尔（亚利桑那州一城市）
Saguaro National Park 仙人掌国家公园
San Antonio 圣安东尼奥（德克萨斯州第二大城市）
Santa Fe 圣达菲（新墨西哥州首府及第四大城市）
Sedona 喜多娜（亚利桑那州一城市）
the Dust Bowl 黄尘地带（20世纪30年代美国南部大平原沙尘暴地区）
the Grand Canyon 大峡谷
the Great Basin 大盆地
the Indian Territory 印第安领地
the National Basketball Association（NBA）美国国家篮球协会
the Palace of the Governors 总督宫（位于新墨西哥州圣达菲市）
Taos 陶斯印第安村（新墨西哥州一城镇）
Tombstone 墓碑镇（亚利桑那州一城镇）
Tucson 图森（亚利桑那州一城市）
Tulsa 塔尔萨（俄克拉何马州第二大城市）
UFO（Unidentified Flying Object）不明飞行物
Will Rogers 威尔·罗杰斯（美国幽默家、演员）

For Fun

Websites to visit

http://www.ok.gov/

　　This is Oklahoma's official website on which you can find information on its government, business, education, etc.

http://www.newmexico.gov/

　　This is a website of New Mexico on which you can find information on its education, health, security, etc.

http://www.texasonline.com/portal/tol

　　This the official website of Texas on which you can find all kinds of information about Texas, such as living, learning, visiting, and working.

http://az.gov/webapp/portal/

　　This is the official website of Arizona, on which you can find all kinds of information about Arizona, such as business, family, health, and safety.

http://en.wikipedia.org/wiki/Roswell_UFO_incident

　　This is a webpage about Roswell UFO incident on which you can find information on its background, cultural influence, etc.

Works to read
Texas (1985)

It is a novel by James A. Michener based on the history of the the Lone Star State. Characters include real and fictional characters, explorers, Spanish and German Texan settlers, ranchers, oil men, aristocrats, Chicanos, and others, all based on extensive historical research. It was made into a movie in 1994.

Movies to see
Oklahoma!

A couple of young cowboys win the hearts of their sweethearts in the Oklahoma territory at the turn of the century, despite the interference of an evil ranch hand and a roaming peddler.

Texas (1941)

Two Virginians are heading for a new life in Texas when they witness a stagecoach being held up. They decide to rob the robbers and make off with the loot. To escape a posse, they split up and do not see each other again for a long time. When they do meet up again, they find themselves on different sides of the law. This leads to the increasing estrangement of the two men, who once thought of themselves as brothers.

Songs to enjoy
"Oklahoma"

"Oklahoma" is the title song from and the finale to the Broadway musical *Oklahoma*! The music and lyrics were written by Richard Rodgers and Oscar Hammerstein II. The melody is reprised in the main title of the 1955 film version and in the overtures of both film and musical productions. The state of Oklahoma officially adopted the song as its state song in 1953.

There's never been a better time to start in life—
It ain't too early and it ain't too late!
Starting as a farmer with a brand new wife—
Soon'll be living in a brand-new state!
Brand new state!
Brand new state, gonna treat you great!
Gonna buy you barley, carrots and pertaters,
Pasture for the cattle, spinach and termaters,
Flowers on the prairie where the June bugs zoom,
Plenty of air and plenty of room,
Plenty of room to swing a rope!

Plenty of heart and
plenty of hope.

Ooook-lahoma, where the wind comes sweepin' down the plain,
And the wavin' wheat can sure smell sweet,
When the wind comes right behind the rain
Ooook-lahoma, Ev'ry night my honey lamb and I,
Sit alone and talk and watch a hawk
Makin' lazy circles in the sky.

We know we belong to the land（yo-ho）
And the land we belong to is grand!
And when we say
Yeeow! Aye-yip-aye-yo-ee-ay!
We're only sayin'
You're doin' fine, Oklahoma!
Oklahoma O.K.!

Ooook-lahoma, where the wind comes sweepin'
down the plain
And the wavin' wheat can sure smell sweet
When the wind comes right behind the rain.
Oklahoma, Ev'ry night my honey lamb and I
Sit alone and talk and watch a hawk
Makin' lazy circles in the sky.

We know we belong to the land
And the land we belong to is grand!
And when we say

Yeeow! Ayipioeeay!
We're only sayin'
You're doin' fine, Oklahoma!
Oklahoma O.K.

Okla-okla-Okla-Okla-Okla-Okla
Okla-okla-Okla-Okla-Okla-Okla...

We know we belong to the land
And the land we belong to is grand!
And when we say
Yeeow! Aye-yip-aye-yo-ee-ay!
We're only sayin'
You're doin' fine, Oklahoma!
Oklahoma
O.K. L-A-H-O-M-A
OKLAHOMA!
Yeeow!

Unit 11

Landform of the Southwest

> This is a great base for tours. People like going to the Grand Canyon. It's like when Americans go to China they have to go to the Great Wall.
>
> —Ken Pontone

Unit Goals

- To have a general idea of the landform of the Southwest
- To learn about the tourist attractions in the Southwest
- To be able to describe the tourist attractions in the Southwest
- To be able to explain why the Sonoran Desert is so dry
- To be able to explain how the Grand Canyon was formed
- To be able to express length, width and height in different ways

Before You Read

1. Here are some animals you are likely to find in the Southwest of the USA. Can you match the names with the animals?
   (rattlesnake, roadrunner, prairie dog, buffalo)

2. The Grand Canyon is located in the state of _____. It is carved by the _____ River, which is swift and sometimes wild, with many _____ and waterfalls.

3. Have you ever heard of Painted Desert? It is located in Northern

Arizona on the _____ Plateau. Do you know who painted the desert? The Nature!

4. Do you know much about cowboys? Match the cowboys' clothing and gear with the names.

horse	to ride so as to drive the cattle
lariat	to rope cattle
boots	to slide into stirrups (narrow-toed)
gloves	to protect hands
hat	to shade eyes and neck
kerchier	to keep dust out of mouth and nose
spurs	to control horse
chaps	to protect legs
bridle	to guide horse (or reins)
woolshirt	to keep warm
saddle	to sit on steadily

5. Form groups of three or four students. Try to find, on the Internet or in the library, more information on tourist attractions in the Southwest which interests you. Prepare a 5-minute classroom presentation.

Start to Read

Text A Desert and Canyon

The Sonoran Desert

The Sonoran Desert in southern Arizona is a very hot and very dry place. It is dry for several reasons. It rains on the average 11 inches each year. The desert is in the **rain shadow** of mountains and most rain that comes nearby falls to the west of the desert. What reaches the desert is mostly dry air. There are no clouds holding moisture in the blue Sonoran Desert sky most of the

time. Without clouds, moisture **evaporates** into the atmosphere easily.

But some plants and animals do survive in the desert. Colorful wildflowers and prickly cactuses grow here. Some cacti grow as tall as four-story buildings. Roadrunners are also visible chasing after a rattlesnake!

The Colorado River and the Grand Canyon

The Colorado River is one of the country's longest rivers. It flows across 1,450 miles of the land and forms part of the Arizona border. The river is swift and sometimes wild, with many rapids and waterfalls. A **bumpy** raft trip down the Colorado is a popular tourist attraction.

The Colorado River carries something else besides people: sand and pebbles. Over millions of years, the **gritty** river water carved away at layer after layer of rock. The river carved deep canyons into the land, forming the greatest canyon of them all, the Grand Canyon.

The Grand Canyon is almost 300 miles long, 18 miles wide at its widest point, and about 1 mile deep. That is four times higher than the Willis Tower in Chicago, once the tallest building in the United States.

The Grand Canyon is also the Earth's history book, recording the changes for about millions of years. Some rocks in the very deepest part of the canyon may be as old as two billion years! Actually, each rock layer is like a book! Near the top is a layer of gray stone that was once the bottom of a warm, shallow sea. This layer is from the age of dinosaurs. Below that you can see footprints from ancient **reptiles** that once walked across hot desert sands. Lower still, even more fossils are visible. Skeletons of some of Earth's oldest plants and animals pressed into the rock are there. At the very bottom of the canyon are traces of ancient mountain ranges.

Text B Plateau, Rivers and Plains

The Colorado Plateau

The Colorado Plateau covers an area of 130,000 square miles (337,000 km²) within western Colorado, northwestern New Mexico, southeastern Utah, and northern Arizona. About 90% of the area is drained by the Colorado River and its main tributaries: the Green, San Juan and Little Colorado. In this region, the land **takes on** some fantastic shapes. Wind and water has eroded the huge Colorado Plateau, forming mesas and buttes, the small, flat-topped landforms and towers of rock. Some rise 1,000 feet straight up. Adding dramatic color to this region is the Painted Desert which is a 150-mile art work of natural beauty with lines of blue, lilac, red and yellow in the rock. The desert is especially beautiful at sunrise and sunset when the colors are the brightest.

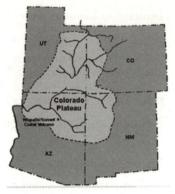

The Rivers

When the snow melts in spring, water **trickles** down the mountains. Brooks flow together to form rivers. The Rio Grande, a big river in the Spanish language, begins in the north in the Rocky Mountains of Colorado. In New Mexico, the river flows out of the mountains. It passes through rugged canyons and onto flat plains as it journeys to the Gulf of Mexico. The 1,240-

mile river forms the border that separates Mexico from Texas and the United States. But for its entire length of 1,885 miles, the Rio Grande provides water for the people, plants, and animals that live along it.

There are other rivers in the Southwest, too. The San Juan and Pecos rivers supply New Mexico with water. The Arkansas River is the main river in Oklahoma. The Red River borders Texas and Oklahoma. Texas has over 5,000 square miles of inland water. The Southwest may be dry, but it is wet too!

The Great Plains

The Great Plains is a vast landform that stretches from south Texas north into Canada. The rolling grassland slopes gently down from the foot of the Rocky Mountains to the woodlands of eastern Oklahoma and Texas.

Thousands of barking prairie dogs built their towns that stretched for miles. Early settlers had to travel all the way around a prairie dog town. Their horses or oxen could break a leg in the prairie dogs' holes.

The Great Plains is the home of grass-loving animals. Huge herds of buffalo used to *roam* the plains. Native Americans and early settlers used to hunt buffalo. In the 1800s, buffalo herds were so thick that they stopped wagon trains for hours! Unfortunately, no one can enjoy the traffic jam nowadays. Heroes like Buffalo Bill killed thousands of buffalos and the herds disappeared forever.

After You Read

Knowledge Focus

1. **Fill in the blanks according to the geographical knowledge you have learned in the text above.**
    (1) _____ is the driest and sunniest region in the USA.
    (2) Part of the _____ desert lies in southern Arizona.
    (3) The Colorado River forms the border between Arizona and _____.
    (4) The _____ River carved deep canyons into the land, forming the greatest canyon of them all, _____.
    (5) The Southwest may be dry, but it is wet too. There are many rivers, such as _____, which borders the United States and Mexico.
    (6) The _____ River borders Texas and Oklahoma.
    (7) _____, the home of grass-loving animals, is a vast landform that stretches from south Texas north into Canada.
    (8) The Colorado Plateau covers an area of 130,000 square miles within western Colorado, southeastern Utah, northern _____, and northwestern _____.

2. **Write T in the brackets if the statement is true and write F if it is false.**
    (1) Because of the desert there, the Southwest is very dry without any waterways. ( )
    (2) In the Sonoran Desert, tourists can see no animals except wildflowers and cactuses. ( )
    (3) The Colorado River is swift and sometimes wild and it is very pretty. ( )
    (4) The Grand Canyon is located in the state of Colorado. ( )
    (5) The Colorado Plateau is drained by the Colorado River and its main tributaries. ( )
    (6) The beauty of the Painted Desert is natural. ( )
    (7) The Rio Grande is a short river that borders Mexico and the USA. ( )
    (8) The Great Plains is a vast landform that stretches from south Texas north into Canada. ( )

3. **Discuss the following questions with your partner.**
    (1) What kind of place is the Southwest of the USA? Give some examples.
    (2) What tourist attractions are there in the Southwest?
    (3) Why is the Sonoran Desert so dry?
    (4) How was the Grand Canyon formed? And what can tourists learn when hiking the Grand Canyon?

Language Focus
1. **Fill in the blanks with the proper forms of the following words or expressions you have learned in the texts.**

bark	take on	press into	herd of
find out	trickle	roam	grass-loving
flat-topped	chase		

   (1) In the Sonoran Desert, you may see a roadrunner _____ after a rattlesnake.
   (2) Hiking down the Grand Canyon, we can read the rocks to _____ about millions of years of Earth's history.
   (3) Each spring the snow melts, and water _____ down the mountains.
   (4) In the Colorado Plateau, the land _____ some marvelous shapes.
   (5) Thousands of _____ prairie dogs built their towns that stretched for miles.
   (6) The Great Plains is the home of _____ animals.
   (7) Once, a large number of buffalo _____ these plains.
   (8) In the 1800s _____ buffalos were so thick that they stopped wagon trains for hours!
   (9) Fossils are skeletons of Earth's oldest plants and animals, _____ rock.
   (10) The small, _____ landforms and towers of rock that were formed are called mesas and buttes.

2. **Fill in the blanks with the proper forms of the words in the brackets.**
   (1) Most of the time, there are no clouds in the blue Sonoran Desert sky. Without clouds, _____ (moist) _____ (evaporation) into the atmosphere.
   (2) _____ (color) wildflowers and _____ (prick) cactuses grow in the desert.
   (3) The Colorado River is _____ (swiftly) and sometimes wild, with many _____ (rapid) and waterfalls.
   (4) A _____ (bump) raft trip down the Colorado is a _____ (popularity) tourist _____ (attract).
   (5) Over millions of years, the _____ (grit) Colorado River water carved away at layer after layer of rock.
   (6) In the Colorado Plateau, the land appears in some _____ (fantasy) shapes.
   (7) The Rio Grande passes through _____ (ruggedness) canyons and onto flat plains as it _____ (journey) to the Gulf of Mexico.
   (8) The entire _____ (long) of the Rio Grande is 1,885 miles.
   (9) The Great Plains is a _____ (vastness) landform that stretches from south Texas north into Canada.

3. **Fill in the blanks with the proper prepositions and adverbs that collocate with the neighboring words.**
   (1) It rains _____ the average 11 inches each year.
   (2) That means that most rain that comes nearby falls _____ the west of the desert. Mostly dry air reaches the desert.
   (3) Clouds hold moisture. Without clouds, moisture evaporates _____ the atmosphere.
   (4) If a skyscraper were built _____ the bottom of the canyon, it would have to be 440 floors high to reach the top.
   (5) Adding dramatic color _____ this region is the Painted Desert.
   (6) The desert is especially beautiful _____ sunrise and sunset when the colors are the brightest.
   (7) The Rio Grande provides water _____ the people, plants, and animals that live along it.
   (8) Thousands of barking prairie dogs built their towns that stretched _____ miles.

4. **How should we express length, width, height, size and age? Try to fill in the following blanks.**
   (1) Some cacti grow as _____ as four-story buildings.
   (2) The Grand Canyon is almost 300 miles _____, 18 miles _____ at its widest point, and about 1 mile _____.
   (3) The Grand Canyon is four times _____ than the Willis Tower, once the tallest building in the USA.
   (4) Some rocks in the very deepest part of the canyon may be as _____ as two billion years!
   (5) But for its entire _____ of 1,885 miles, the Rio Grande provides water for the

people, plants, and animals that live along it.

(6) The Mississippi River runs 6,400 kilometers _____.

(7) The Delmarva Peninsula is almost 300 _____ 100 km or about 180 _____ 60 miles.

(8) The glaciers were 10,000 feet _____ and thousands of miles _____.

Comprehensive Work

1. Group Work: Making Generalizations

Unit 11 describes the southwestern landform of the United States. You are expected to have four generalizations about the Southwest America below. Write two or three examples that support each generalization. Then write your own generalization about the Southwest America and provide examples to support it. At last, present your points of view to your partner, and have a discussion. Remember that a generalization is a kind of conclusion or rule that applies to many examples. Generalizations use words such as *all*, *many*, *some*, *generally*, and *never*.

Generalizations

(1) Some landforms in the Southwest are very large.

Examples

(2) Rivers in the Southwest serve many purposes.

Examples

(3) Most of the Southwest is landlocked.

Examples

(4) My own generalization: _____

_____

Examples

2. Solo Work: Surf the Internet for some information about the Rio Grande and one of the big rivers in the Southwest of China. Write a composition, comparing and contrasting them.

Read More

Text C — Drought in the Southwest

Read the passage quickly and circle the meaning of the following words or phrases in the passage.

(1) in tight supply (Para. 1)
    A. short of supply   B. full of supply   C. running out

(2) stretched (Para. 2)
    A. caused to become longer   B. used beyond its limits   C. straightened

(3) alter (Para. 3)
    A. reduce   B. control   C. change

(4) aridity (Para. 4)
    A. deficiency of moisture   B. vitality   C. diversity

(5) parched (Para. 5)
    A. dried out   B. patched   C. fertile

(6) withdraw (Para. 8)
    A. keep away from others   B. cause to be returned   C. retire gracefully

Changing climate will mean increasing drought in the American Southwest—a region where water already is **in tight supply**—according to a new study.

"The bottom line message for the average person and also for the states and federal government is that they'd better start planning for a Southwest region in which the water resources are increasingly **stretched**," said Richard Seager of Columbia University's Lamont Doherty Earth Observatory.

Seager is lead author of the study published online Thursday by the journal *Science*. Researchers studied 19 computer models of the climate, using data dating back to 1860 and projecting into the future, to the year 2100. The same models were used in preparing the reports of the Intergovernmental Panel on Climate Change. The consensus of the models was that climate in the southwestern United States and parts of northern Mexico began a transition to drier conditions late in the 20th century and is continuing the trend in this century, as climate change **alters** the movement of storms and moisture in the atmosphere. The models show the drying trend continuing all the way to 2100—for more than 90 years.

"If these models are correct, the levels of **aridity** of the recent multiyear drought, or the Dust Bowl and 1950s droughts, will, within the coming years to decades, become the new climatology of the American Southwest," the researchers wrote.

In a telephone interview, Seager said that doesn't mean there would be dust storms like those of the 1930s Dust Bowl, because conditions at that time were also complicated by poor agricultural practices. But he said the reduction in rainfall could be equivalent to those times when thousands of farmers abandoned their **parched** land and moved away in search of jobs.

Currently, the majority of water in the Southwest is used in agriculture, but the urban population of the region is growing and so the water needs of people are growing as well, he explained.

"So, in a case where there is a reduced water supply, there will have to be some reallocation between the users," Seager said. "The water available is already fully allocated."

He said feels that adjustments can be made to deal with the change, perhaps by **withdrawing** some land from production and by conserving water in urban areas.

"But it's something that needs to be planned for," Seager said. "It's time to start thinking how to deal with that."

Proper Names

Buffalo Bill 野牛比尔
Columbia University's Lamont Doherty Earth Observatory 哥伦比亚大学拉蒙特多尔蒂地球观测站
Mexicans 墨西哥人
Richard Seager 理查德·西格
Science 《科学》(杂志)
the American Southwest 美国西南部
the Arkansas River 阿肯色河
the Civil War (美国)内战
the Colorado Plateau 科罗拉多高原
the Colorado Plateaus Province 科罗拉多省
the Colorado River 科罗拉多河
the Green (River) 格林河

the Gulf of Mexico 墨西哥湾
the Intergovernmental Panel on Climate Change 联合国政府间气候变化工作小组
the Little Colorado 小科罗拉多河
The Modern Ranch 《现代农场》
the Painted Desert 派提德沙漠(又译"多色沙漠""多彩沙漠",位于亚利桑那州北部)
the Pecos River 佩科斯河
the Red River 红河
the Rio Grande 格兰德河
the San Juan (River) 圣胡安河
the Sonoran Desert 索诺兰沙漠
Utah 犹他州

For Fun

Websites to visit

http://www.pima.gov/cmo/sdcp/kids/

This is a website about the Sonoran Desert in simple English, on which you can find information of the animals, plants, cultures, etc.

http://www.grandcanyon.com/

This is a comprehensive website of the Grand Canyon, on which you can find such information as maps, park information, camping, weather, etc.

Works to read
Grand Canyon National Park (A Natural History Guide)

The Grand Canyon is perhaps the most awesome sight in the United States—and one of the wonders of the world. Much of the park's beauty is related to its geology and ecology. Schmidt explores the shape of the land, its plants and animals, and its human history. This is a fascinating book that everyone visiting the Grand Canyon should read.

Movies to see
Red River

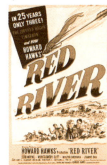

Red River is a 1948 Western film giving a fictional account of the first cattle drive from Texas to Kansas along the Chisholm Trail. The dramatic tension stems from a growing feud over the management of the drive, between the Texas rancher who initiated it (John Wayne) and his adopted adult son (Montgomery Clift).

Songs to enjoy
"Mamas Don't Let Your Babies Grow Up to Be Cowboys"

It is a country music song written by Ed Bruce and Patsy Bruce. It was made famous by Waylon Jennings and Willie Nelson, whose version was first released on their 1978 album *Waylon & Willie*. The song's lyrics advise mothers to raise their children as doctors or lawyers rather than cowboys, who seem to be "always alone."

Mama don't let your babies grow up to be cowboys
Don't let 'em pick guitars and drive them old trucks
Make 'em be doctors and lawyers and such
Mama don't let your babies grow up to be cowboys
They'll never stay home and they're always alone
Even with someone they love
Cowboys ain't easy to love and they're harder to hold
And they'd rather give you a song than diamonds or gold
Lonestar belt buckles and old faded Levi's each night
Begins a new day
And if you don't understand him and he don't die young
He'll probably just ride away

Mama don't let your babies grow up to be cowboys
Don't let 'em pick guitars and drive them old trucks
Make 'em be doctors and lawyers and such
Mama don't let your babies grow up to be cowboys
They'll never stay home and they're always alone
Even with someone they love
Cowboys like smoky old pool rooms and clear mountain morinin's
Little warm puppies and children and girls of the night
And them that don't know him won't like him
And them that do sometimes won't know how to take him
He ain't wrong he's just different
But his pride won't let him do things to make you think he's right

Mama don't let your babies grow up to be cowboys
Don't let 'em pick guitars and drive them old trucks
Make 'em be doctors and lawyers and such
Mama don't let your babies grow up to be cowboys
They'll never stay home and they're always alone

Even with someone they love
Mama don't let your babies grow up to be cowboys
Don't let 'em pick guitars and drive them old trucks
Make 'em be doctors and lawyers and such

Unit 12

View of the West

> Go West, young man, and grow up with the Country.
> —John Babsone Soule

Unit Goals

- To have a general idea of the landform of the West
- To be able to describe the landform of the West
- To be able to tell who were the first men to visit the Rockies and why
- To be able to use past participles more skillfully

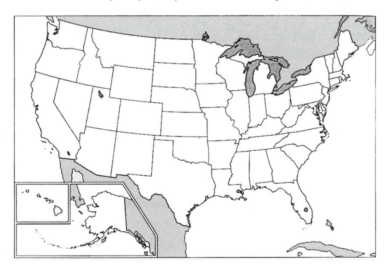

Before You Read

1. What states are there in the West of the USA? Can you locate and label, on the map above, the states in the West—Montana, Wyoming, Colorado, Utah, Nevada, Idaho, Washington, Oregon, California, Alaska and Hawaii?

127

2. Do you still remember the Rocky Mountains? The Rocky Mountains are also called _____. They are located in the _____ of the USA.
3. We have already learned the Great Lakes, located in the North of America. In the West, there is also a great lake—the Great _____, located in the state of _____.
4. Have you ever heard of a landform in the West with the word "death" in its name? Yes, that is _____ in the state of _____.
5. What tourist attractions in California do the following photos show?

6. Form groups of three or four students. Try to find, on the Internet or in the library, more information on tourist attractions in the West which interests you. Prepare a 5-minute classroom presentation.

Start to Read

Text A The Rocky Mountains, Clear Rivers and Salty Lakes

The Rocky Mountains

The vast Mountains and Desert region was a land which people hurried through on their way west seeking land and gold. The settlers found neither at first until they reached the Pacific slopes. But later, gold was found at Pikes Peak and in a few other parts of the Rocky Mountains.

Unit 12   View of the West

The high, sharp, rugged, **majestic** Rocky Mountains stretch all the way from Mexico to the Arctic. Compared with the Appalachians in the East, they are young and their faces of bare rock are **capped with** snow, even to the south. In the high valleys, there are remains of glaciers while below them are clear, icy lakes made by the glaciers.

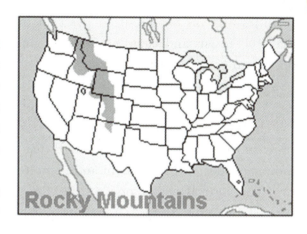

The first white men to visit the mountains were Spanish explorers, moving across the southern ranges to the Pacific. Stories of gold took them there, but they did not stay. No one stayed—not even the hunters who roamed the northern ranges. Until little more than a century ago, the Rockies seemed almost impossible to cross. But gold rush makes the impossible possible. After 1848, when gold was found in the river beds of California, great numbers of people crossed the mountains over trails discovered by the hunters. Today, eight railroads and a dozen highways go winding over the mountains, following routes made by these settlers and **prospectors**.

In the days when gold was king and thousands of men lived in the mining camps in the wilderness, agriculture started in the Rockies. Most of the farmers were Mormons—or Latter-Day Saints as they called themselves. After experiencing many years of **intolerance** in the East where their sect was founded, they traveled west under the leadership of Brigham Young. They sought a **secluded** valley and finally found it near the waters of the Great Salt Lake, in what was to become the State of Utah.

The ancient waters that brought soil to these mountain valleys had no way of reaching the sea, so they spread out in shallow lakes. As the water slowly evaporated, minerals remained in the lake beds. The Great Salt Lake, for example, contains an estimated six thousand million tons of salt. Another lake holds millions of tons of soda. The lakes change size and shape with the rainfall and sometimes dry up completely in arid weather.

In this land of little water, farming was very difficult. It would have been impossible without a series of irrigation canals that bring water from the high mountain streams to the dry valleys below.

The water that is brought down the mountains is stored in two natural lakes—Utah Lake and Bear Lake—and six man-made **storage** facilities. These facilities **account for** about 75 per cent of the total water in the states. More than 100 towns and **countless** gardens now **flourish** in this region which had once been considered **worthless**.

Clear Rivers and Salty Lakes

In the Rocky Mountains, it snows through the fall and winter and it can snow in August. In spring, when all that snow melts, water **tumbles** down the mountainsides. Streams form and come together to form rivers.

The Bear River is one of the rivers formed by snow water. It begins nearly 13,000 feet up in the mountains and ends only 90 miles away, but it has dropped about 9,000 feet!

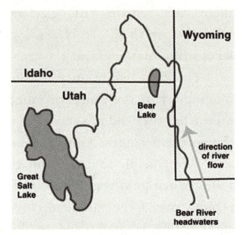

Nearly all rivers **eventually empty** into the sea, but not the Bear River. This river flows into the Great Salt Lake, the largest lake in the West. The rivers and streams that flow into the lake bring with them about two million tons of salt each year. And no fresh water drains away from the lake. Instead, the summer sun evaporates the fresh water, leaving the salt behind. The lake water is so salty that people do not sink in it!

Text B — **Hottest, Driest, and Highest**

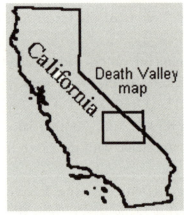

Death Valley in sunny southern California is trapped between towering mountain ranges. Native Americans call this valley "ground on fire." It deserves the name for it can reach over 115°F. On a summer day, the air is usually around 100°F in the shade. **To top it off**, the average rainfall is less than two inches a year.

Can life survive in such a hot and dry environment? The answer is **affirmative**. At night, when the temperature goes down, coyotes, owls, and snakes are as active as you can imagine.

Here is also the highest mountain peak in the contiguous states. The top of Mt. Whitney is 14,494 feet above the sea level. Since it is above the timberline, it is too high for trees go grow. There is usually snow even in the middle of summer!

After You Read

Knowledge Focus

1. **Fill in the blanks according to the geographical knowledge you have learned in the texts above.**
   (1) The Rocky Mountains stretch all the way from _____ to the _____.
   (2) After 1848, when _____ was found in the river beds of _____, great numbers of people crossed the mountains over trails discovered by the hunters.
   (3) Death Valley is in sunny southern _____.
   (4) _____ contains an estimated six thousand million tons of salt.
   (5) _____ starts from Utah, flows through _____ and Idaho, and ends in the Great Salt Lake in _____.
   (6) The top of Mt. Whitney is above the _____, where it is too high for trees to grow.
   (7) _____ and _____ are not the states of the continental USA.

2. **Write T in the brackets if the statement is true and write F if it is false.**
   (1) Compared with the Appalachians in the East, the Rockies are young. ( )
   (2) The first white men to visit the Rockies were Spanish explorers. ( )
   (3) The west is wet since it has so many lakes. ( )
   (4) The Bear River flows through several states and finally empties into the sea. ( )
   (5) Death Valley is located in the state of California and it is very hot. ( )
   (6) Death Valley is so named because no animals could live there. ( )
   (7) Mt. Whitney is the highest mountain peak in the USA. ( )

Language Focus

1. **Fill in the blanks with the proper forms of the following words or expressions you have learned in the texts.**

excavate	flourish	roam	to top it off
evaporate	compare with	tumble	empty into
account for			

   (1) Nearly all rivers finally _____ the sea.
   (2) In spring, when all that snow melts, water _____ down the mountainsides.
   (3) These facilities _____ about 75 per cent of the total water in the states.
   (4) _____ the Appalachians in the East, the Rockies are young and their faces of bare rock are capped with snow, even to the south.
   (5) A series of irrigation canals are frequently _____ through rock.
   (6) The summer sun _____ the fresh water, leaving the salt behind.
   (7) No one stayed—not even the hunters who _____ the northern ranges.
   (8) It is very hot even in the shade. _____, the average rainfall is less than two inches a year.
   (9) More than 100 towns and many gardens now _____ in this region which had once been considered valueless.

2. **Fill in the blanks with the proper forms of the words in the brackets.**

   (1) The first white men to visit the mountains were _____ (explore) form _____ (Spanish), moving across the southern ranges to the Pacific.
   (2) Until about a century ago, the Rockies seemed _____ (possible) to cross; but the chance of finding gold in the state of California makes men do _____ (probable) things.
   (3) There are eight railroads and a dozen highways over the mountains, following routes made by these settlers and _____ (prospect).
   (4) After experiencing many years of _____ (tolerant) in the East, Mormons traveled west under the leadership of Brigham Young.
   (5) They sought a _____ (seclusion) valley and finally found it near the waters of the Great Salt Lake.
   (6) The water that is brought down the mountains is stored in two natural lakes and six man-made _____ (store) facilities.
   (7) More than 100 towns and _____ (count) gardens now thrive in this region which had once been considered _____ (worth).
   (8) Nearly all rivers _____ (event) go into the sea.
   (9) Mt. Whitney is the highest peak in the _____ (contiguity) states.
   (10) The _____ (majesty) Rocky Mountains are all high, sharp and rugged.

3. **Fill in the blanks with the proper prepositions and adverbs that collocate with the neighboring words.**

   (1) The Rockies are capped with snow, even _____ the south.

(2) They traveled west _____ the leadership of Brigham Young.
(3) The ancient waters have no way _____ reaching the sea.
(4) The lakes sometimes completely dry up _____ arid weather.
(5) Native Americans call this valley "ground _____ fire."
(6) It is too high for trees to grow. That means that the top of mountain is _____ the timberline.

4. **Change the following complex sentences into simple sentences by using the past participles.**
   (1) When they are compared with the Appalachians in the East, the Rockies are young.
   (2) Below the remains are clear, icy lakes which were made by the glaciers.
   (3) Great numbers of people crossed the mountains over trails which had been discovered by the hunters.
   (4) Today, eight railroads and a dozen highways go winding over the mountains, following routes which were made by the settlers and prospectors.
   (5) It is estimated that the Great Salt Lake contains six thousand million tons of salt.
   (6) The Bear River is one of the rivers which were formed by snow water.

Comprehensive Work

1. **Pair Work:** Draw a picture or a map about the landform of the West. Then show and explain it to your partner.

2. **Solo Work:** Try to write a poem about one of the landforms in the West and share it with your classmates.

Read More

Text C   Bear River Course

Read the passage quickly and fill in the following blanks.
(1) The Bear River is the longest river in North America not draining into _____.
(2) The Bear River circles through three states, Wyoming, Utah and _____, but starts and ends in _____.
(3) Today, the Bear River enters the Bear Lake Valley north of Bear Lake. It flows _____, following the Bear Lake fault along the eastern edge of the Bear Lake Valley and no longer flows directly into _____, except through a man-made channel created in 1912.
(4) About 140,000 years ago, Erosion of one lava dam probably allowed the Bear River to drain _____ again but another lava flow about 80,000 years ago returned the river to _____ where it remains today.

The Bear River is the longest river in North America not draining into an ocean. It circles through three states, Wyoming, Utah and Idaho, but starts and ends in Utah. The past movements of the Bear River are important to our understanding of Bear Lake, in part because the volume of water in the river can rapidly change lake levels, and because the river water chemistry is very different than the lake chemistry. Today, the Bear River enters the Bear Lake Valley north of Bear Lake. It flows northward, following the Bear Lake fault (断层) along the eastern edge of the Bear Lake Valley and no longer flows directly into Bear Lake, except through a man-made channel created in 1912.

About 140,000 years ago, lava flows from near Soda Springs, Idaho blocked the Bear River channel and diverted the river into the Great Basin. Erosion of the lava dam probably allowed the Bear River to drain oceanward again but another lava flow about 80,000 years ago returned the river to the Great Basin where it remains today. Some time after that, a large lake formed in Bear Lake Valley, possible due to landslides damming the north end of the valley near Georgetown, Idaho. The Bear River then flowed into the larger lake, changing the chemistry of the water and creating beaches and other shoreline features 25—200 feet above the level of today's lake.

Proper Names

Alaska 阿拉斯加州
Brigham Young 杨百翰(耶稣基督后期圣徒教会首领,率领耶稣基督后期圣徒教会的教友长途跋涉来到盐湖城并定居下来)
California 加利福尼亚州
Cascade Mountains 卡斯克德山
Death Valley 死谷
Georgetown 乔治城(爱达荷州一城市)
Hawaii 夏威夷州
Idaho 爱达荷州
Latter-Day Saints 末世圣徒(即摩门教徒)
Montana 蒙大拿州
Mormons 摩门教徒
Mt. Whitney 惠特妮山峰
Nevada 内华达州
Oregon 俄勒冈州

Pikes Peak 派克斯峰
Soda Springs 苏打泉
the Alps 阿尔卑斯山脉
the Arctic 北极
the Bear Lake 贝尔湖
the Bear River 贝尔河(熊河)
the Coast Ranges 海岸群山
the Columbia Plateau 哥伦比亚高原
the Great Salt Lake 大盐湖
the Pyramid Lake 金字塔湖
the Sierras 内华达山脉
the Snake River Plain 蛇河平原
the Wasatch Mountains 瓦萨奇山脉
the West 美国西部
Utah Lake 犹他湖
Wyoming 怀俄明州

For Fun

Websites to visit

http://www.rocky.mountain.national-park.com/

This is the Rocky Mountain National Park page, on which you can find all kinds of information about the Rocky Mountain National Park such as lodging, maps, camping, tours, and pictures.

http://www.deathvalley.com

This is a comprehensive website of Death Valley, on which you can find information of its lodging, camping, resources, news, etc.

Works to read

McTeague by Frank Norris

First published in 1899, it is set in San Francisco. The protagonist is a simple dentist named McTeague. The narrator never reveals McTeague's first name; he is referred to only as "Mac" by the other characters in the novel. In Erich von Stroheim's film adaptation, *Greed*, his first name is said to be John at one point, but there is no basis for this in the novel. The novel was also the basis of an opera by Robert Altman, William Bolcom, and Arnold Weinstein.

Movies to see

Death Valley (1982)

A divorced mother, her young son and her new boyfriend set out on a road trip through Death Valley and run afoul of a local serial killer.

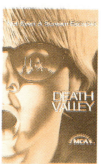

Rocky Mountain (1950)

A Confederate troop, led by Captain Lafe Barstow, is prowling the far ranges of California and Nevada in a last desperate attempt to build up an army in the West for the faltering Confederacy. Because the patrol saves a stagecoach, with Johanna Carter as one of the passengers, from an Indian attack, and is marooned on a rocky mountain, it fails in its mission but the honor of the Old South is upheld.

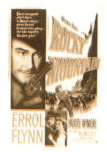

Flica (2006)

In this home-on-the-range tale, 16-year-old Katy dreams of growing up to work on her father's Wyoming ranch. Her dad, however, would rather see her leave the ranch and go to college. When Katy finds a wild mustang, Flicka, and tries to tame the horse for

riding, she takes on an even bigger struggle than the one with her father.

Songs to enjoy

"Death Valley Nights" by Blue Oyster Cult

Bleached by the sun	Desolate landscapes
And scorned by the moon	Storybook bliss
If I make it 'til tomorrow noon	Darling let me tell you
I'm leaving	This is crazy
'Tween the horror of space	Hell of a memory
And the terror of time	Is a Heaven a pain
My heart in crystal	Snow is cold but so is rain
Down the line I'm screaming	Please save me
What I need is a kiss from you babe	What I need is a kiss from you babe
Before it's hangover time	Before it's hangover time
What I need is some love from you babe	What I need is some love from you babe
Before this stampede arrives	Before the stampede arrives
	I need you

Unit 13

Temples of Nature and Cities of the Pacific

> There is nothing so American as our national parks.... The fundamental idea behind the parks... is that the country belongs to the people, that it is in process of making for the enrichment of the lives of all of us.
>
> —Franklin D. Roosevelt

Unit Goals

- To have a general idea of the national parks in the West
- To be familiar with the cities of the Pacific
- To be able to describe how the oldest national park came into being
- To be able to introduce Yellowstone National Park and San Francisco

Before You Read

1. _____ National Park is the first national park in the USA. It is located in the northeast corner of the state of _____. Most visitors there want to get a look at _____, the world's famous geyser.
2. Since the bears roam free, visitors to the park often meet them. If you hike in Yellowstone, what would you do in order not to encounter them? Go with a _____ and make lots of _____. You may even want to wear "bear _____" around your ankles. This way the bears know you're coming!
3. Here are two kinds of animals in Yellowstone National Park. Do you know their names?

4. _____, nicknamed "the city by the bay," lies on a tip of land between Pacific Ocean and San Francisco Bay in the state of _____.
5. _____, nicknamed "The Emerald City," is located in the state of _____.
6. Form groups of three or four students. Try to find, on the Internet or in the library, more information on Yellowstone National Park or any coastal cities in the West which interests you. Prepare a 5-minute classroom presentation.

Start to Read

Text A　　Temples of Nature

When the first miners and hunters returned from the Rocky Mountains, they brought back such **marvelous** tales of natural beauty that a group of scientists decided to test the truth of their stories. These **skeptical** scientists, who visited the Rockies in 1870, wrote reports that sounded more like fiction than fact. They described a mountain made entirely of black glass, rivers of ice that were blue-white, magnificent deep canyons, towering white waterfalls, and great caves far beneath the earth.

One night, as the members of the party rested around their campfire, they discuss ways of preserving these magnificent natural scenes. It was finally and enthusiastically agreed that the whole area should be **set aside** as a great national park for all people to enjoy. This suggestion was accepted by the federal government and, two years later, Yellowstone National Park **came into being**. Today some 9,000 square kilometers of this **magnificent** wilderness are **preserved** for millions of visitors to enjoy. Since 1872, the system of national parks has grown **steadily**. By 1973, there were 38 areas set aside by the national government. State and local governments have added smaller regions.

The land in the national parks belongs to the federal government which

Unit 13 *Temples of Nature and Cities of the Pacific*

bought the areas from the states or private individuals. The government protects the plants and animals native to each national park area. No rancher, miner, hunter or logger may use its meadows, trees or wildlife, except under strict controls.

The parks are under the **jurisdiction** of the National Park Service, whose **rangers** protect the areas, guide visitors through the parks, and lecture on the natural phenomena so that the visitor can more fully enjoy the natural monuments, scenery, wild animals and plants. Within the parks, there are campgrounds, cabins and motels **available** to the approximately 180 million annual visitors.

Yellowstone is still the favorite of tourists. Excellent highways lead into the park. Comfortable, inexpensive lodgings are offered. Experienced instructors serve as guides to the famed geysers and hot springs and animals wander about unhunted and unafraid.

Some parks are famous for their scenery; others have special significance for students of geology or cultural anthropology. For example, Mesa Verde National Park is a tableland about 24 kilometers long and 13 kilometers wide, rising 600 meters out of the valley below. It contains the cliff **dwellings** of some of America's earliest known Indian tribes. Rocky Mountain National Park is a geological museum which contains the remains of older mountains, canyons, forests and glaciers. Yosemite National Park is famous for its beauty: its waterfalls which **cascade** 730 meters, and its valleys which have walls over 900 meters high.

But perhaps no scene can equal the Grand Canyon of the Colorado. There, for a million and a half years, the great river has been gouging through the mountain rocks. The most impressive parts of the canyon lie within the 270-square-kilometer Grand Canyon National Park.

More than any other section of the United States, the mountains and deserts are still the country of immense open space. This land, which once barred the way of **weary** travelers, now has become a land for winter and summer vacation, a land of magic and wonder.

Text B Cities of the Pacific

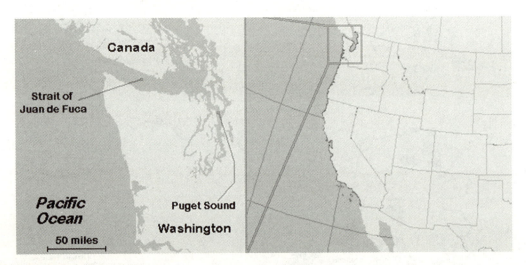

Just as the natural Harbors of New England are America's door to Europe, the shores of Puget Sound open the way to the Orient. Thousands of years ago, a glacier moved south from the Canadian mountains and dug out the valley floor of Puget Sound. Sea floods poured in when the ice melted, creating a blue-green inland sea, guarded east and west by snow-capped mountains. Between these ocean-filled valleys, there are wooded peninsulas and islands, with hundreds of waterways and natural harbors. South of the sound, tall cones of **extinct** volcanoes rise 2,400 meters into the air from great mountain plateaus.

Many manufacturing and fishing towns lie along the **forested** hills and lowlands that **flank** the bays and inlets of the northwest coast. At cities like

Seattle, Portland, Everett, Tacoma, Bellingham and Olympia, goods from Asia and the South Pacific are unloaded while fruit, grain, fish, condensed milk in cans, timber or machines are put aboard ships **bound** for ports all over the world. The waters of Puget Sound itself are crowded with small fleets of fishing boats and houseboats afloat or anchored along the shore.

About 1,400 kilometers south of Seattle, San Francisco lies at the tip of a tongue of land broken by the narrow channel of the Golden Gate. Through this channel the tides of the Pacific pour into a great bay. The city has long been a center of commerce, finance, shipping and culture for more than three million people in the metropolitan bay area. Asians and **successive** waves of Europeans have made San Francisco multilingual and multicultural. Freight from a hundred ports is unloaded at a fine **landlocked**
harbor, while long lines of railroad cars bring into the city the fruit of the Central Valley. The transcontinental railroad connects San Francisco with the industrial and agricultural centers of the Midwest and the East, thus providing an interchange of goods and passengers. And the city's airport, one of the largest in the United States, accommodates close to a total of 400,000 landings and takeoffs a year. Great streams of motor traffic cross the Golden Gate Bridge, 1.6 kilometers long, to the north shore.

Less than a decade after the beginning of the 20th century, this major metropolis of the West was in ruins. In 1906, a great earthquake shook the city to its foundations and a great fire completed the destruction. But within three years, a new city had risen out of the ashes of the old.

After You Read

Knowledge Focus

1. **Fill in the blanks according to the geographical knowledge you have learned in the texts above.**

   (1) Yellowstone National Park came into being in the year of _____.

   (2) Yellowstone National Park is located in the state of _____.

   (3) The land in the national parks belongs to _____ which bought the areas from the states or private individuals.

   (4) Yosemite National Park is located in the state of _____.

(5) Just as the natural Harbors of New England are America's door to Europe, the shores of _____ open the way to the Orient.

(6) About 1,400 kilometers south of Seattle, _____ lies at the tip of a tongue of land broken by the narrow channel of the Golden Gate.

(7) In 1906, a great _____ shook San Francisco to its foundations and a great _____ completed the destruction.

(8) Sacramento is the capital of the state of _____.

2. **Write T in the brackets if the statement is true and write F if it is false.**

(1) Establishing a national park is a way of preserving the magnificent natural scenes for all people to enjoy. ( )

(2) The lands in the national park belong to the local government. ( )

(3) Within the parks, there is no campground or motel available to the visitors, so they have to take sleeping bags with them. ( )

(4) Seattle is located in Washington in the West of the USA. ( )

(5) Las Vegas is the largest city in the state of Nevada and it is famous for gambling. ( )

(6) Los Angeles is the largest city in California, often abbreviated as L.A. ( )

(7) San Diego is located along the Pacific Ocean on the West coast of the Western United States. ( )

(8) San Francisco has not yet recovered from the damage caused by the earthquake in 1906. ( )

Language Focus

1. **Fill in the blanks with the proper forms of the following expressions you have learned in the texts.**

just as	lecture on	set...aside	bound for
available to	dig out	sound like	come into being
close to	belong to		

(1) The reports _____ fiction more than fact.

(2) The whole area should be _____ as a great national park for all people to enjoy.

(3) Yellowstone National Park _____ two years later.

(4) The land in the national parks _____ the federal government.

(5) The rangers _____ the natural phenomena so that the visitor can more fully enjoy the natural monuments, scenery, wild animals and plants.

(6) Within the parks, some facilities are _____ the visitors.

(7) Thousands of years ago, a glacier moved south from the Canadian mountains and _____ the valley floor of Puget Sound.

(8) _____ the natural Harbors of New England are America's door to Europe, the shores of Puget Sound open the way to the Orient.

(9) Fruit, grain, fish, and condensed milk in cans, timber or machines are put

aboard ships _____ ports all over the world.

(10) San Francisco's airport accommodates _____ a total of 400,000 landings and takeoffs a year.

2. **Fill in the blanks with the proper forms of the words in the brackets.**

(1) These _____ (skepticism) scientists, who visited the Rockies in 1870, wrote reports that sounded more like _____ (fictional) than fact.

(2) The miners and hunters brought back such _____ (marvel) tales of _____ (nature) beauty that a group of scientists decided to test the _____ (true) of their stories.

(3) The system of _____ (nation) parks has grown _____ (steady).

(4) The parks are under the _____ (juridical) of the National Park Service.

(5) The Grand Canyon once stopped the _____ (wear) travelers.

(6) There are _____ (approximate) 180 million annual visitors to the parks.

(7) Comfortable and _____ (expensive) lodgings are offered in Yellowstone National Park.

(8) Some parks have special significance for students of geology or cultural _____ (anthropological).

(9) Mesa Verde National Park contains the cliff _____ (dwell) of some of America's earliest known Indian _____ (tribal).

(10) The waters of Puget Sound itself are crowded with small fleets of fishing boats and houseboats _____ (float) or _____ (anchor) along the shore.

(11) Many fishing towns lie along the _____ (forest) hills and lowlands.

(12) Asians and _____ (succession) waves of Europeans have made San Francisco multilingual and multicultural.

(13) The transcontinental railroad provides an _____ (change) of goods and passengers.

(14) The city has long been a center of _____ (commercial), finance, culture for millions of people in the _____ (metropolis) bay area.

3. **Fill in the blanks with proper prepositions and adverbs that collocate with the neighboring words.**

(1) The government protects the plants and animals native _____ each national park area.

(2) The parks are _____ the jurisdiction of the National Service.

(3) The shores of Puget Sound open the way _____ the Orient.

(4) Tall cones of extinct volcanoes rise 2,400 meters _____ the air from great mountain plateaus.

(5) San Francisco lies _____ the tip of a tongue of land broken by the channel.

(6) The major metropolis of the West was _____ ruins.

(7) In 1906, a great earthquake shook the city _____ its foundation.

(8) Within three years, new city had risen _____ of the ashes of the old.

4. Discuss with your partner what the object of the highlighted verb is in each of the following sentences.

(1) Long lines of railroad cars **bring** into the city the fruit of the Central Valley.

(2) The great northern ice flowed over the North American continent and **ground** into it a number of major changes.

(3) Into this area of industry came millions of Europeans who **made** of it what became known as the "melting pot."

(4) We must always **keep** alive the memory of what we have learnt.

(5) You are so angry. Why don't you try to be calm and **explain** to me what has happened?

(6) Plastic heart valves and other human "spare parts" have **made** possible many recent developments in surgery.

(7) The Chinese government has **made** clear what it strives to achieve in space science in the next 5 years.

(8) Our research **brings** to light unsettling facts that you have a right to know.

Comprehensive Work

1. **Solo Work**: Recite the second paragraph about Yellowstone National Park in the text. See who can be the first one in the class to retell it from memory.

2. **Solo Work**: Have you ever heard of any national park in China? What impresses you most in the park? Write a composition, comparing it with Yellowstone.

Read More

Text C   Yellowstone National Park

Read the passage quickly and fill in the following blanks.

(1) Yellowstone is located in the northwest corner of _____.

(2) Old Faithful is so named probably because _____
_____.

(3) In Yellowstone National Park, visitors may see some large animals such as _____
_____.

Yellowstone National Park covers more than 809 million square meters in the northwest corner of Wyoming. It is a special for more than just its size. Established in 1872, it is the oldest national park in the world. More importantly, it is home to natural wonders and fascinating wildlife.

Most visitors to Yellowstone want to get a look at Old Faithful, the world's most famous geyser, a natural hot spring that shoots out steam and boiling water. About every 80 minutes, Old Faithful's plume of stream gushes 55 meters into the air!

Yellowstone is home to herds of elk and buffalo. Buffalo are the largest animals in the park. Adults can grow as big as 1,135 kilograms. Both black and grizzly bears live in Yellowstone. The bears roam free in the park and they can be dangerous to visitors when they are surprised. That is why visitors are advised to go with a group and make lots of noise. Wearing "bear bells" around one's ankles serves as another way of self-protection, informing the bears of the coming visitors.

Proper Names

Bellingham 贝林翰(华盛顿州一城市)
Everett 埃弗雷特(华盛顿州一城市)
Grand Canyon National Park 大峡谷国家公园
Lake Washington 华盛顿湖
Lombard Street 朗伯德街
Mesa Verde National Park 梅莎维德国家公园
Mount Rainier 雷尼尔山
Nob Hill 诺布山
Old Faithful 老忠实泉
Olympia 奥林匹亚(华盛顿州首府)
Portland 波特兰(俄勒冈州西北部港市)
Puget Sound 普格特海峡/普吉特海湾
Rocky Mountain National Park 落基山国家公园
Russian Hill 俄罗斯山
San Francisco 旧金山(加利福尼亚州一重要城市)
San Francisco Bay 旧金山湾
Seattle 西雅图(华盛顿州一主要城市)
Tacoma 塔科马(华盛顿州西部港市)

the Cable Car Museum 缆车博物馆
the Canadian mountains 加拿大山脉
the Cascade Mountain Range 喀斯喀特山脉
the Central Valley 中央谷
the Emerald City 翡翠城(西雅图市的别称)
the Golden Gate (Strait) 金门海峡
the Golden Gate Bridge 金门大桥
the Lake Washington Ship Canal 华盛顿湖大运河
the Midwest 美国中西部
the National Park Service 国家公园管理局
the Olympic Mountains 奥林匹亚山
the Orient 东方诸国
the Pacific Northwest 太平洋西北部
the South Pacific 南太平洋
the Yukon 育空(加拿大一个地区)
Yellowstone National Park 黄石国家公园
Yosemite National Park 优胜美地/约塞米蒂国家公园

For Fun

Websites to visit

http://www.nps.gov/

  This is a comprehensive website of the national parks in the USA, on which you can find all kinds of information on the national parks, such as nature, science, history, culture, etc.

http://www.enchantedlearning.com/usa/states/california/

  This is a webpage of California, on which you can find all kinds of information about California.

Works to read

Fear and Loathing in Las Vegas by Hunter S. Thompson

  It is a novel by Hunter S. Thompson, illustrated by Ralph Steadman. The story follows its protagonist, Raoul Duke, and his attorney, Dr. Gonzo, as they descend on Las Vegas to chase the American Dream through a drug-induced haze. The novel first appeared as a two-part series in *Rolling Stone* magazine in 1971. It was later adapted into the 1998 film of the same name starring Johnny Depp and Benicio del Toro.

Beautiful Children by Charles Bock

  Fearless, empathetic, all-encompassing in scope, Charles Bock's debut novel delivers a masterful panorama of Las Vegas and the web of lonely children and suffering adults who struggle under its glimmering lights—homeless teenagers, strippers, comic book illustrators, pawn brokers, musicians, video store clerks. At the center of this rich Dickensian universe is a missing boy, and the search for him leads to a swirling climax of heartache and brittle redemption.

Movies to see

Yellowstone

  It is a 63-minute 1936 film directed by Arthur Lubin and starring Judith Barrett, Henry Hunter, Raymond Hatton, and Andy Devine, combining murder mystery, romance, and natural setting.

San Francisco

It is a 1936 drama-adventure film directed by Woody Van Dyke, based on the April 18, 1906 San Francisco earthquake. The film, which was the top grossing movie of that year, stars Clark Gable, Jeanette MacDonald, and Spencer Tracy.

Getting There

This film is about Mary-Kate and Ashley turning sixteen years old and going on a road trip without parents. They are headed to Utah for the Olympics and arrive late. There are also scenes in Las Vegas. The twins do not drive alone in this movie, they take a bus.

Songs to enjoy

"Seattle"

Music by Hugo Montenegro/Lyrics by Ernie Sheldon, Jack Keller / Performed by Perry Como

The bluest skies you've ever seen are in Seattle
And the hills the greenest green, in Seattle
Like a beautiful child, growing up, free an' wild

Full of hopes an' full of fears, full of laughter, full of tears
Full of dreams to last the years, in Seattle
...in Seattle!

When it's time to leave your home and your loved ones
It's the hardest thing a boy can ever do
An' you pray that you will find someone warm an' sweet an' kind
But you're not sure what's waiting there for you!

The bluest skies you've ever seen are in Seattle
And the hills the greenest green, in Seattle
Like a beautiful child, growing up, free an' wild

Full of hopes an' full of fears, full of laughter, full of tears
Full of dreams to last the years, in Seattle
...in Seattle!

When you find your own true love, you will know it
By her smile, by the look in her eye
Scent of pine trees in the air, never knew a day so fair
It makes you feel so proud that you could cry!

The bluest skies you've ever seen are in Seattle
And the hills the greenest green, in Seattle
Like a beautiful child, growing up, free an' wild

Full of hopes an' full of fears, full of laughter, full of tears
Full of dreams to last the years, in Seattle
...in Seattle!

In Seattle...in Seattle...in Seattle!

"L. A." by Neil Young

In a matter of time,
There'll be a friend of mine
Gonna come to the coast,
You're gonna see him
Up close for a minute or two
While the ground cracks under you.
By the look in your eyes
You'd think that it was a surprise
But you seem to forget
Something somebody said
About the bubbles in the sea
And an ocean full of trees.

And you now, L. A.
Uptight,
city in the smog,
city in the smog.
Don't you wish that
you could be here too?
Don't you wish that
you could be here too?
Don't you wish that
you could be here too?

Well, it's hard to believe
So you get up to leave
And you laugh at the door
That you heard it all before
Oh it's so good to know
That it's all just a show for you.

But when the suppers are planned
And the freeways are crammed
And the mountains erupt
And the valley is sucked
Into cracks in the earth
Will I finally be heard by you.

L. A.
Uptight,
city in the smog,
city in the smog.
Don't you wish that
you could be here too?
Don't you wish that
you could be here too?
Don't you wish that
you could be here too?

Unit 14

Newest States

> To the lover of wilderness, Alaska is one of the most wonderful countries in the world.
> —John Muir

Unit Goals

- To have a general idea about the newest states of the USA
- To be able to describe the features of the newest states of the USA
- To be able to contrast Alaska & Hawaii from different aspects
- To be able to use "it," "one" and "that" properly

Before You Read

1. _____ and _____ are the two newest states of the USA.
2. Match the terms that are more closely connected.

                                    the Bering Sea
Alaska   Canada
                                    US Pacific Fleet
                                    Honolulu
Hawaii   Arctic Circle
                                    Pearl Harbor
                                    Juneau
                                    Captain Cook

3. _____, the largest state of the USA, is located in the _____ of the North American Continent. To the east lies another country— _____.
4. _____, the newest state of the USA, is located on an archipelago in the central _____ Ocean southwest of the continental United States, southeast of Japan, and northeast of Australia.

5. Do you know the state flower of Alaska? Look at the photo on the right. Its name is made up of three English words. It is _____.

6. Form groups of three or four students. Try to find, on the Internet or in the library, more information on Alaska or Hawaii, which interests you. Prepare a 5-minute classroom presentation.

Start to Read

Text A Alaska

In 1959, Americans welcomed Alaska into the Union as the 49th state, **symbolizing** a change of attitude from that held in 1867, when the peninsula was **purchased** from Russia. Then, most Americans had little interest in the 1,500,000 square kilometers "of icebergs and polar bears"—beyond Canada's western borders, far from the settled areas of the United States.

In those sections of the state which lie above the Arctic Circle, Alaska still is a land of icebergs and polar bears. Ice masses lie buried in the earth, which is **permanently** frozen to a depth of 90 or more meters. From early May until early August, the midnight sun never sets on this flat, treeless region, but the sun cannot melt the icy soil more than two-thirds of a meter down.

Alaska is America's largest state, but only about 325,000 people live there. According to estimates, 800,000 hectares of its land area are fit for plowing but only about 640,000 hectares are being **cultivated**.

The Japan Current of the Pacific warms Alaska, and the Arctic chills it. The temperature may **drop** as low as minus 43 degrees centigrade in some places, and may rise to 30 degrees. In any given year, more than 11 meters of snow may fall in the north, and more than two meters of rainfall may **descend** upon the city of Juneau in the South.

Alaska lies between about 71 degrees and 56 degrees north latitude, stretching southward from the Arctic Ocean to the Pacific. This **immense** peninsula is sharply divided into three distinct regions. In the north, Arctic Alaska reaches from the Arctic Ocean to the steep glacier-cut peaks of the Brooks Range. Central Alaska lies between the Brooks Range and the Alaska Range, where Mount McKinley rises 6,187 meters—the highest peak in North America. From the western face of the Alaska Range, the mainland slopes down toward the Bering Sea and Russia, and the island chain of the Aleutians **extends** far to the southwest. The 640-kilometer strip of coastal land known as the "Panhandle of Alaska" thrusts to the southeast, bordering Canada's Province of British Columbia.

Arctic Alaska has been the home to Eskimos for **countless** centuries. It is believed that Eskimos moved there from Mongolia or Siberia, probably crossing Bering Strait, named for Vitus Bering, the Danish sea captain who discovered Alaska on his voyage for Russia in 1741. The Eskimos—the Aleuts of the southeast—are the state's earliest known inhabitants. Russian fur traders established settlements but, by the time Alaska was sold to the United States, most of the traders had **departed**.

Then in 1896, gold was discovered near the Klondike River in Canada just across the Alaska border. Thousands of Americans rushed to the region on their way to the Klondike; some never left Alaska, and some returned there after the region experienced a "rush" of its own.

Alaska was never completely **cut off** again, although even today transportation is a major problem. There are only two motor routes from the US mainland, and within the state, roads and railroads are relatively limited though nearly every town has its own airfield. Planes fly passengers, mail and freight to the most distant villages.

The gold rush that changed life so suddenly for Alaska was soon ended, and although many stories about mining camps have become part of American literature, the gold from Alaskan earth contributed less to economic progress than the fish from Alaskan waters. The fish caught in a single year range in value from $80 million to $90 million. Fur-**bearing** animals are plentiful in the forests and streams, and valuable fur seals **inhabit** the waters. Since 1911, Canada, Japan, Russia and the United States have jointly agreed to control the hunting of seals. The herd has been rebuilt to its former size of about 1.5 million.

After fishing, the state's chief industry is lumber and the production of wood pulp. There are also large **deposits** of oil—due to be brought to the mainland by a 1,280-kilometer pipeline—coal, copper, gold and other important minerals.

After You Read

Knowledge Focus

1. **Fill in the blanks according to the geographical knowledge you have learned in the text above.**

    (1) In 1959, Americans welcomed _____ into the Union as the 49th state.

    (2) _____ is America's largest state, but only about 325,000 people live there.

(3) The Japan Current of _____ warms Alaska, and the Arctic chills it.
(4) _____ in the Central Alaska is the highest peak in North America.
(5) Arctic Alaska has been the home to _____ for many centuries. It is believed that _____ moved to Alaska from Mongolia or Siberia.
(6) Then in 1896, _____ was discovered near the Klondike River in Canada just across the Alaska border. Thousands of Americans rushed to the region on their way to the Klondike.
(7) _____ from Alaskan earth contributed less to economic progress than _____ from Alaskan waters.
(8) After fishing, the state's chief industry is _____ and the production of _____.

2. **Rearrange the following sentences in time order.**
   ____ (1) Americans welcomed Alaska into the Union as the 49th state.
   ____ (2) Vitus Bering, the Danish sea captain, discovered Alaska on his voyage for Russia.
   ____ (3) Gold was discovered near the Klondike River in Canada just across the Alaska border.
   ____ (4) Canada, Japan, Russia and the United States jointly agreed to control the hunting of seals.

Language Focus

1. **Fill in the blanks with the proper forms of the following words or expressions you have learned in the text.**

welcome…into	depart	rush to	fit for
descend upon	cut…off	have little	interest in
inhabit	cultivate		

(1) In 1959, Americans _____ Alaska _____ the Union as the 49th state.
(2) Then, most Americans _____ the 1,500,000 square kilometers "of icebergs and polar bears."
(3) More than two meters of rainfall may _____ the city of Juneau in the South.
(4) 800,000 hectares of its land area are _____ plowing but only about 640,000 hectares are _____.
(5) By the time Alaska was sold to the United States, most of the traders _____.
(6) Alaska was never completely _____ again, although even today transportation is a major problem.
(7) Fur-bearing animals are plentiful in the forests and streams, and valuable fur seals _____ the waters.
(8) Thousands of Americans _____ the region on their way to the Klondike; some never left Alaska, and some returned there after the region experienced a "rush" of its own.

2. Fill in the blanks with the proper forms of the words in the brackets.
  (1) From early May until August, the midnight sun never sets on this flat, _____ (tree) region, but the sun cannot melt the icy soil more than two-thirds of a meter down.
  (2) Arctic Alaska has been the home to Eskimos for _____ (count) centuries.
  (3) The Eskimos—the Aleuts of the southeast—are the state's earliest known _____ (inhabit).
  (4) _____ (Russia) fur _____ (trade) established settlements but, by the time Alaska was sold to the United States, most of the traders had _____ (departure).
  (5) In those sections of the state which lie above the Arctic Circle, Alaska still is a land of icebergs and _____ (pole) bears.
  (6) There are also large _____ (deposit) of oil, coal, copper, gold and other important _____ (mine).
  (7) In any given year, more than 11 meters of snow may fall in the north, and more than two meters of rainfall may _____ (descent) upon the city of Juneau in the South.
  (8) Fur-bearing animals are _____ (plenty) in the forests and streams and valuable fur seals _____ (inhabitation) the water.
  (9) From the western face of the Alaska Range, the mainland slopes down toward the Bering Sea and Russia, and the island chain of the Aleutians _____ (extension) far to the southwest.
  (10) The gold from _____ (Alaska) earth _____ (contribution) less to _____ (economy) progress than the fish from _____ (Alaska) waters.

3. Fill in the blanks with proper prepositions and adverbs that collocate with the neighboring words.
  (1) Alaska is _____ Canada's western borders, far _____ the settled areas of the United States.
  (2) In those sections of the state which lie _____ the Arctic Circle, Alaska still is a land of icebergs and polar bears.
  (3) Arctic Alaska has been the home _____ Eskimos for countless centuries.
  (4) Ice masses lie buried in the earth, which is frozen _____ a depth of 90 or more meters.
  (5) The gold from Alaskan earth contributed less _____ economic progress than the fish fro Alaskan waters.
  (6) The fish caught in a single year range _____ value from $80 million to $90 million.
  (7) Alaska lies _____ about 71 degrees and 56 degrees north latitude.
  (8) This immense peninsula is sharply divided _____ three distinct regions.

4. Fill in the blanks with the proper forms of "it," "one" or "that."
  (1) In 1959, Americans welcomed Alaska into the Union as the 49th state, symbolizing a change of attitude from _____ held in 1867.

(2) In their experience and _____ of their fathers, the only good soil was soil in which trees grow.
(3) _____ is believed that Eskimos moved there from Mongolia or Siberia.
(4) Mary's handwriting is far better than _____ of Peter.
(5) A chair made of steel is stronger than _____ made of wood.
(6) Waves of red light are about twice as long as _____ of blue light.
(7) His ideas are little different from _____ of his friends.
(8) We can lend you plastic chairs or metal _____.

Comprehensive Work
Pair Work:
(1) American government plans to subsidize some college students to visit Alaska so as to better understand it. Students need to write a proposal. List the reasons that may come into your proposal. And then share your reasons with your partner.

_____

_____

_____

(2) If you shall stay in Alaska for 24 hours in your winter holiday this year, and you can only take 5 things with you, what will you choose? List your choices and the reasons. And then share your information with your partner.

Choices	Reasons
a. _____	_____
b. _____	_____
c. _____	_____
d. _____	_____
e. _____	_____

Read More

Text B   Hawaii

Scan the passage for the right answer to the following questions.
(1) 1778 is the year that _____ discovered Hawaii.
   A. James Cook   B. Missionaries   C. Polynesian voyagers
(2) The population of Hawaii is _____.
   A. 16,700   B. 845,000   C. 3,200 million

(3) _____ of the population came from Europe or America.

　　A. About five sixths　　B. Most　　C. About one sixth

(4) Hawaii has _____ major island(s).

　　A. eight　　B. five　　C. one

(5) Which of the following is NOT true?

　　A. Hawaii is located in the tropical zone, and it is very hot.

　　B. The average temperature is about 24°F.

　　C. The ocean currents and the winds cool the temperature, so the climate is comfortable.

(6) _____ is the world's largest active volcano.

　　A. Kilauea　　B. Mauna Loa　　C. Waialeale

(7) Honolulu, _____, is located on _____.

　　A. capital of Hawaii, Molokai　　B. largest city of Hawaii, Kauai

　　C. capital of Hawaii, Oahu

(8) The most important crop in Hawaii is _____.

　　A. pineapple　　B. sulfur　　C. sugar

　　In the fifth or sixth century A.D., **daring** Polynesian voyagers in outrigger canoes sailed to Hawaii across thousands of kilometers of the Pacific and are believed to have been the island's first inhabitants. Not until British Captain James Cook **accidentally** landed there in 1778 did the world learn of Hawaii's existence. Traders, planters and **missionaries** soon followed.

　　About 845,000 people inhabit the island chain's land area of 16,700 square kilometers. By origin, they are most closely related to the countries of Asia and the Pacific—chiefly Japan, the Philippines, China and Korea—while only about one-sixth of the population originated in Europe or America. Politically, Hawaiians have been related to the United States since 1900 when, as a result of their request for American citizenship, their former kingdom became an organized territory. In 1959, the territory was admitted to the Union as the 50th state —a state separated from the mainland by about 3,200 kilometers of ocean.

　　The eight major islands and over 100 small islets of Hawaii—like a chain of beads some 2,575 kilometers long—lie upon the Pacific, southeast to northwest. Although the state is located in the tropical zone, its climate is comfortable because of the ocean currents that pass its shores and the winds that blow across the land from the northeast. The temperature usually remains close to the annual average of 24 degrees centigrade.

Rough, black rocks of lava jut out of the water along parts of the coastline. In some places, cliffs rise almost straight up from the water's edge. Along the gently sloping land areas to the southeast are beaches of yellow, white and black sands.

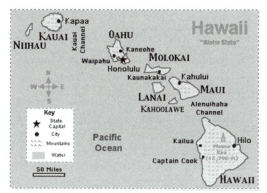

The largest land, Hawaii, lies at the southeastern end of the chain and is almost twice as large as all the others combined. Five volcanoes gave the island its form; two are still active: Kilauea and Mauna Loa. Mauna Loa, the world's largest active volcano, towers above the scenic Hawaiian National Park which stretches from the 4,250-meter mountain peak across the sea to neighboring Maui, the valley island. Topical plants, sandy desert, waterfalls, craters and caves make the 780-square-kilometer park a tourist attraction.

The best known of all the islands is the third largest, Oahu. A diamond-shaped **plot** of earth no more than 64 kilometers long and 42 kilometers wide, it is the center of Hawaiian life. Honolulu, capital, largest city and home to more than half of all Hawaiians, spreads out over 218 square kilometers of land at the foot of the volcanic Koolau mountain range. Eleven kilometers away lies

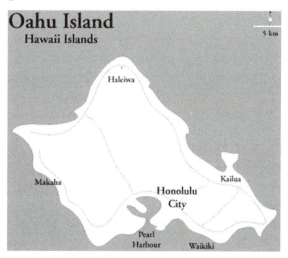

Pearl Harbor, where the US Pacific Fleet is based. Waikiki Beach, enjoyed by Hawaii's kings in ancient times and by world visitors today, extends along the shore from Honolulu to Diamond Head, an extinct volcano.

Honolulu's harbor is a port of call for more than 1,000 ships a year, and the international airport, with nearly a half-million flights a year, is the busiest in the Pacific. About 2,260,000 people visit the island every year and provide more than $890 million of Hawaii's annual income.

Although the islands are world famous for their thrilling scenery, each major member of the chain has its distinctive character. On green Kauai, probably the oldest, is Mount Waialeale, an extinct volcano and one of the rainiest places on earth with an average annual precipitation of 1170 centimeters.

Molokai has two main agricultural regions: the dry western plateau dotted with cattle ranches, and a fertile central plain, home of pineapple farms. Lanai, once thinly blanketed with dry, brown grass, now is one vast pineapple plantation. Perhaps more pure-blooded Hawaiians live in Niihau's 187 square kilometers than in any other part of the chain. Kahoolawe, close to Maui, is barren, waterless, and uninhabited.

The rich volcanic soil of the islands has been made to flourish through scientific agriculture and man-made waterways. Hawaii's farm workers are among the highest paid in the world. Although there are no fuel resources and few useful minerals except sulfur, there are many industries, and Honolulu alone makes more than 160 different kinds of products.

The first official ties between Hawaii and the United States were created through trade in sugar. In 1876, the United States granted tax-free entry to Hawaiian sugar and thereby helped its cultivation. Today, 17 sugar companies cultivate more than 96,000 hectares of sugarcane on four of the islands.

Pineapple, the second most important crop, is grown on five islands on a total area of more than 25,000 hectares. Other important crops include coffee, fruit and vegetables.

Text C Hawaii, a Time Travel Dream

by Blushfulmoon

Read the poem and discuss the following questions with your partner.
(1) What words describe the poet's anxiety to go back to Hawaii?
(2) What trees does the poet want to see in Hawaii?
(3) What words of color does the poet use in this poem? What are their functions?
(4) Can you find two lines rhymed in each stanza?

I'd like to travel back in time to Hawaii
It keeps calling my name, invading my brain
Flooding me with feeling
Of aching and pain～

I want to see the ocean breezes, Polynesian places
Palm trees swaying in the wind
Azure blue waters, spun white sparkling sands
And a tropical drink in my hand～

I want to sip on a pina colada
See Ponce de Leon the blood thirsty pirate
With his jewels and treasures on the beach
Bright diamond skies, parrot lullabies
Breathe in exotic Hawaiian flowers
Tempting blooms just out of reach～

I want to see the mango trees, coconut groves
And sugar cane plantations
Nights of soft-scented winds
Vivid luau's, hula dancers
Not re-enactments, the real creation～
Dark ocean waves, near scary coves and caves
Watching a volcano spewing sulfuric breezes
Gaze on the untamed land, entranced by it's spell
Engrossed in the real history
As restless natives yell～

Sometime later I wake up, look over my suitcases are packed
Slowly I drink Kona Coffee with cream
Now awake, not disoriented or fuzzy
I realize and sigh
It hadn't happened yet
It was only a dream～

Proper Names

Alaska 阿拉斯加州
Aleutians 阿留申群岛
Diamond Head 钻石山（火山）
Eskimos 爱斯基摩人
Captain James Cook 杰姆士·库克船长
Hawaii 夏威夷
Honolulu 檀香山（又译"火奴鲁鲁"，夏威夷州首府）
Kahoolawe 卡胡拉维岛（夏威夷群岛中的一个岛屿）
Kauai 考艾岛（夏威夷群岛中的一个岛屿）
Kilauea 基罗亚火山
Kona Coffee 科纳咖啡
Lanai 拉奈岛（夏威夷群岛中的一个岛屿）
Maui 茂伊岛（夏威夷群岛中的一个岛屿）
Mauna Loa 蒙纳洛火山
Molokai 摩罗凯岛（夏威夷群岛中的一个岛屿）
Mongolia 蒙古
Mount McKinley 麦金莱山
Mount Waialeale 外阿勒阿山
Niihau 尼豪岛（夏威夷群岛中的一个岛屿）
Oahu 欧胡岛（夏威夷群岛中的一个岛屿）
Pearl Harbor 珍珠港
Polynesian 波利尼西亚的
Siberia 西伯利亚
the Aleuts 阿留申人
the Alaska Range 阿拉斯加山脉
the Arctic Circle 北极圈
the Bering Sea 白令海
the Bering Strait 白令海峡
the Brooks Range 布鲁克斯山脉
the Klondike River 克朗代克河
the Koolau Mountain Range 库劳山脉
the North American Continent 北美大陆
the Philippines 菲律宾
the US Pacific Fleet 美国太平洋舰队
Vitus Bering 威图斯·白令（丹麦航海家）
Waikiki Beach 怀基基海滩

For Fun

Websites to visit

http://www.travelalaska.com/

It is a website about traveling in Alaska, on which you can find all kinds of information, such as things to do and places to visit.

http://www.hawaii.com/ and http://www.gohawaii.com/

These two are both comprehensive websites of Hawaii, on which you can find all kinds of information about this state, such as its islands, what to do and where to stay.

Works to read

Alaska by James A. Michener

In this sweeping epic of the northernmost American frontier, James A. Michener guides us across Alaska's fierce terrain, from the long-forgotten past to the bustling technological present, as his characters struggle for survival. The exciting high points of Alaska's story, from its brutal prehistory, through the nineteenth century and the American acquisition, to its modern status as America's thriving forty-ninth state, are brought vividly to life in this remarkable novel.

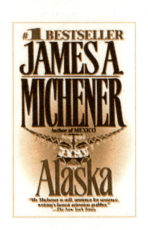

Hawaii by James A. Michener

It is a novel by James A. Michener published in 1959. Written in episodic format, like most of Michener's works, the book narrates the story of the original Hawaiians, who sailed to the islands from Bora Bora, the early American missionaries and merchants, and the Chinese and Japanese immigrants who traveled to work and seek their fortunes in Hawaii. The story begins in the 800s and ends in the mid-1950s.

Movies to see

Alaska

It is a 1996 film directed by Fraser Clarke Heston.

Jake Barnes and his two kids, Sean and Jessie, have moved to Alaska after his wife dies. He is a former airline pilot now delivering toilet paper across the mountains. During an emergency delivery in a storm his plane goes down somewhere in the mountains. Annoyed that the authorities are not doing enough, Jessie and Sean set out on an adventure to find their father with the help of a polar bear which they have saved from a ferocious poacher.

To Brave Alaska

It is an American 1996 television film directed by Bruce Pittman. The film was released on DVD first in Asia.

A newlywed couple decides to move to Alaska to live in the wilderness. Caught by a violent storm while they are hundreds of miles away from the nearest town, the couple is forced to turn their weaknesses into strengths in order to survive. They have no one else to depend on except for themselves.

Hawaii

It is a 1966 American film based on the novel of the same name by James A. Michener. It tells the story of an 1820s Yale University divinity student (Max von Sydow) who, along with his new bride (Julie Andrews), becomes a Calvinist missionary in the Hawaiian Islands.

Pearl Harbor

The classic story of the Japanese attack on Pearl Harbor is told through the eyes of two boyhood friends, now serving as officers in the Army Air Corps. Rafe is an energetic young pilot who is selected to fly with the British in Europe while America is still not at war. After Rafe is shot down and presumed killed, however, Danny comforts Rafe's former lover, Evelyn, and the two draw closer. But, when Rafe turns up alive, the two former friends become enemies, and it is through the turmoil of Pearl Harbor that the two may reconcile their differences.

Songs to enjoy

"Alaska and Me" by John Denver

When I was a child and I lived in the city
I dreamed of Alaska so far away
And I dreamed I was flying over mountains and glaciers
Somehow I knew I'd live there one day
Well it took me some growin', and a fair bit of schoolin'
And a little bit of trouble to get on the move
And I felt like a loser but I turned out the winner
When I came to Alaska the land that I love

Here's to Alaska, here's to the people
Here's to the wild and here's to the free
Here's to my life in a chosen country
Here's to Alaska and me

I was born in a cabin on Little Mulchatna
Raised in hard times but I had a good life
From the first time I flew with my father a singin'
I knew that I'd wind up a bush pilot's wife
We sleep near the sound of a slow running river
And wake up most mornings to a drizzling rain
And we face every day like the first or the last one
With nothin' to lose and heaven to gain

Here's to Alaska, here's to the people
Here's to the wild and here's to the free
Here's to my life in a chosen country
Here's to Alaska and me

Oh, for the fire on a cold winters night
And once more to gaze at the great northern lights
For all of the beauty my children will see
Here's to Alaska and me
Here's to Alaska, here's to the people
Here's to the wild and here's to the free
Here's to my life in a chosen country
Here's to Alaska and me

"Blue Hawaii" written by Leo Robin and Ralph Rainger

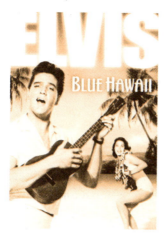

(Artist: Elvis Presley)

Night and you and Blue Hawaii
The night is heavenly and you are heaven to me

Lovely you and Blue Hawaii
With all this loveliness there should be love

Come with me while the moon is on the sea
The night is young and so are we, so are we

Dreams come true in Blue Hawaii
And mine could all come true this magic night of nights with you

Come with me while the moon is on the sea (the moon is on the sea)
The night is young and so are we (so are we)

Dreams come true in Blue Hawaii
And mine could all come true this magic night of nights with you

Unit 15

Review: Regions of the USA

> This is America ... a brilliant diversity spread like stars, like a thousand points of light in a broad and peaceful sky.
> —George W. Bush

Unit Goals

- To have a summary about the five regions in the USA
- To reinforce the useful geographical terms about the different regions
- To learn the highlighted useful words and expressions that describe the regional differences in the USA
- To improve English language skills

Before You Read

Which region is the statement about, the Northeast, the Southeast, the Midwest, the Southwest, or the West?

(1) There are top-ranking universities and colleges that are people's pride. _____
(2) It houses the nation's largest city, its financial hub, and its cultural center. _____
(3) Crops grow easily in its soil and can be grown without frost for at least six months of the year. _____
(4) It has a lot of "belts," such as a Manufacturing Belt, a Dairy belt, a Wheat Belt and a Corn Belt. _____
(5) It has strong Spanish-American and Native-American components, and outside the cities, the region is a land of open spaces, much of which is desert. _____
(6) It is regarded as the last frontier. _____

Unit 15 Review: Regions of the USA

Start to Read

Text A   New England, Mid-Atlantic, Southeast and Midwest

Americans often speak of their country as one of several large regions. These regions are cultural units rather than governmental units—formed by history and geography and shaped by the economics, literature and folkways that all the parts of a region share. What makes one region different from another? A region's multicultural heritage as well as distinct **demographic** characteristics like age and occupation makes it different and special. Within several regions, language is used differently and there are strong dialects. There are also differences in outlook and attitude **based on** geography.

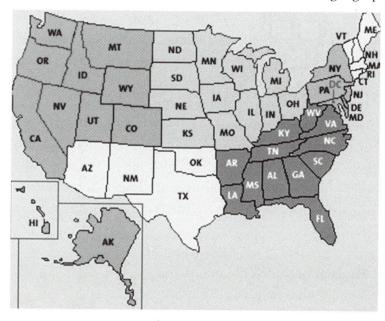

New England

New England (Connecticut, Maine, Massachusetts, New Hampshire, Rhode Island, Vermont) has played a **dominant** role in American history. Until well into the 19th century, New England was the country's cultural and economic center. The earliest

European settlers of New England were English **Protestants** who came in search of religious liberty. They gave the region its **distinctive** political format—town meetings (an outgrowth of meetings held by church elders) in which citizens gathered to discuss issues of the day.

Town meetings still function in many New England communities today and have been **revived** as a form of dialogue in the national political arena. New England is also important for the cultural contribution it has made to the nation. The critic Van Wyck Brooks called the creation of a distinctive American literature, in the first half of the 19th century, "the flowering of New England." Education is another of the region's strongest legacies. The cluster of top-ranking universities and colleges in New England — including Harvard, Yale, Brown, Dartmouth, Wellesley, Smith, Williams, Amherst, and Wesleyan— is unequaled by any other region. America's first college, Harvard, was founded at Cambridge, Massachusetts in 1636.

Without, however, large expanses of rich farmland or a mild climate, generations of **exasperated** New England farmers declared that the chief product of their land was stones. By 1750, many settlers had turned from farming to other **pursuits**. In their business dealings, New Englanders gained a reputation for hard work, **shrewdness**, thrift, and **ingenuity**.

Mid-Atlantic

If New England provided the brains and dollars for the 19th century American expansion, the Mid-Atlantic states (Delaware, Maryland, New Jersey, New York, Pennsylvania, Washington, D.C.) provided the muscle. The region's largest states, New York and Pennsylvania, became centers of heavy industry (iron, glass, and steel). The Mid-Atlantic region was settled by a wider range of people than New England. Into this area of industry came millions of Europeans who made of it what became known as the "melting pot." As heavy industry spread throughout the region, rivers such as the Hudson and Delaware were **transformed** into vital shipping lanes. Cities on waterways—New York on the Hudson, Philadelphia on the Delaware, Baltimore on Chesapeake Bay—grew **dramatically**. New York is still the nation's largest city, its financial hub, and its cultural center. But even today, the visitor who expects only factories and crowded cities is surprised. In the Mid-Atlantic, there are more wooded hills than factory chimneys, more fields than concrete roads, and more farmhouses than office buildings.

The Southeast

The Southeast (Alabama, Arkansas, Florida, Georgia, Kentucky, Louisiana, Mississippi, North Carolina, South Carolina, Tennessee, Virginia, West Virginia) is perhaps the most distinctive region of the United States region. The American Civil War (1861—1865) devastated the Old South socially and economically. Slavery was the issue that divided North and South. To northerners, it was immoral; to southerners, it was **integral** to their way of life and their plantation system of agriculture. The scars left by the war took decades to heal. The **abolition** of slavery failed to **provide** African Americans **with** political or economic equality; and it took a long, concerted effort to end **segregation**. The "New South" has **evolved into** a manufacturing region and high-rise buildings crowd the skylines of such cities as Atlanta and Little Rock. The region, however, still has many landscapes to delight the human sense of poetry and wonder. The region **is blessed with** plentiful rainfall and a mild climate. Crops grow easily in its soil and can be grown without frost for at least six months of the year. Owing to its mild weather, the South has become a mecca for retirees from other regions.

The Midwest

The Midwest (Illinois, Indiana, Iowa, Kansas, Michigan, Minnesota, Missouri, Nebraska, North Dakota, Ohio, South Dakota, Wisconsin) is known as the nation's "breadbasket." The fertile soil of the region makes it possible for farmers to produce abundant harvests of cereal crops such as wheat, oats, and corn. Corn is the most important of all American crops, as basic to American agriculture as iron is to American industry. The annual crop is greater than the nation's yield of wheat, rice and other grains combined. On hot, still midsummer nights in the Corn Belt, farmers **insist** they can hear the corn growing.

Farms are normally located separate from each other, close to the fields, and often **beyond** the sight of its neighbors. The village or town is principally a place where the farm family travels to buy supplies, to attend church and to go for **entertainment** or political, social or business meetings. Midwesterners are praised as being open, friendly, and straightforward. Their politics tend to be cautious, but the caution is sometimes **peppered** with protest.

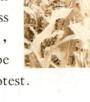

After You Read

Knowledge Focus

1. **Fill in the blanks according to the geographical knowledge you have learned in the text above.**
   (1) The earliest European settlers of _____ were English Protestants who came in search of religious liberty.
   (2) America's first college, _____, was founded at Cambridge, _____ in 1636.
   (3) If New England provided the brains and dollars for the 19th century American expansion, the _____ states provided the muscle.
   (4) The Mid-Atlantic region's largest states, _____ and _____, became centers of heavy industry (iron, glass, and steel). Into this area of industry, came millions of Europeans who made of it what became known as the _____.
   (5) The nation's largest city is still _____.
   (6) The _____ has evolved into a manufacturing region and high-rise buildings crowd the skylines of such cities as Atlanta and Little Rock.
   (7) The _____ is blessed with plentiful rainfall and a mild climate.
   (8) _____ are praised as being open, friendly, and straightforward.

2. **Write T in the brackets if the statement is true and write F if it is false.**
   (1) Americans often speak of their country as one of several large regions. These regions are governmental units rather than cultural units. ( )
   (2) Until well into the 19th century, New England was the country's cultural and

economic center. （ ）

(3) Within several regions, language is used differently and there are strong dialects, but no differences in outlook and attitude based on geography. （ ）
(4) Maryland is located in New England. （ ）
(5) In the Mid-Atlantic, there are more wooded hills than factory chimneys, more fields than concrete roads, and more farmhouses than office buildings. （ ）
(6) Slavery was the issue that divided North and South. To southerners, it was immoral. （ ）
(7) The abolition of slavery failed to provide African Americans with political or economic equality. （ ）
(8) Corn is the most important of all American crops. （ ）

Language Focus

1. Fill in the blanks with the following words or expressions you have learned in the text.

revive	in search of	exasperate	insist
be blessed with	base on	provide with	evolve into
concerted	devastate		

(1) There are also differences in outlook and attitude _____ geography.
(2) Town meetings have been _____ as a form of dialogue in the national political arena.
(3) I was _____ by all the delays.
(4) The "New South" has _____ a manufacturing region.
(5) The abolition of slavery failed to _____ African Americans _____ political or economic equality.
(6) The region _____ plentiful rainfall and a mild climate.
(7) It took a long, _____ effort to end segregation.
(8) On hot, still midsummer nights in the Corn Belt, farmers _____ they can hear the corn growing.
(9) The American Civil War (1861—1865) _____ the Old South socially and economically.
(10) He went _____ his long-lost brother.

2. Fill in the blanks with the proper forms of the words in the brackets.
(1) New England has played a _____ (domain) role in American history.
(2) A region's multicultural heritage as well as distinct _____ (demography) characteristics makes it different and special.
(3) They gave the region its _____ (distinct) political format—town meetings.
(4) By 1750, many settlers had turned from farming to other _____ (pursue).
(5) In the Mid-Atlantic, there are more _____ (wood) hills than factory chimneys.
(6) _____ (slave) was the issue that divided the North and South.
(7) In their business dealings, New Englanders gained a reputation for hard work,

_____ (shrewd), thrift, and ingenuity.

(8) New England is important for the cultural _____ (contribute) it has made to the nation.

3. Fill in the blanks with the proper prepositions and adverbs that collocate with the neighboring words.

(1) As heavy industry spread throughout the region, rivers such as the Hudson and Delaware were transformed _____ vital shipping lanes.

(2) Town meetings still function _____ many New England communities today.

(3) Owing _____ its mild weather, the South has become a mecca for retirees _____ other regions.

(4) Corn is the most important of all American crops, _____ basic to American agriculture as iron is to American industry.

(5) Farms are normally located separate from each other, close to the fields, and often _____ the sight of its neighbors.

(6) _____ this area of industry came millions of Europeans who made of it what became known as the "melting pot."

(7) To northerners, it was immoral; to southerners, it was integral _____ their way of life and their plantation system of agriculture.

(8) _____ several regions, language is used differently and there are strong dialects.

Comprehensive Work

1. **Solo Work:** Mark the five major regions of the USA in different colors on the outline map below.

2. **Pair Work**: Select the terms that are more closely connected and share your selection with your partner.

    the Corn Belt   New York City on the Hudson
    a mecca for retirees   Harvard, Yale
    English Protestants   plentiful rainfall and a mild climate
    the nation's breadbasket   the melting pot
    New England: _____
    Mid-Atlantic: _____
    Southeast: _____
    Midwest: _____

3. **Group Work**: Form groups of three or four. Discuss the following questions with your group members and then present your group's idea in class.

(1) Which region/city in China is like a melting pot? Why?

The melting pot in China	Reasons
	1.
	2.
	3.

(2) Which region/city in China is like a mecca for retirees? Why?

The mecca for retirees in China	Reasons
	1.
	2.
	3.

Read More

Text B   **The Southwest**

Read the passage quickly and decide if the statements are true or false accordingly. Write T if it is true, and write F if it is false.

(1) The Southwest is drier than the adjoining Midwest in weather and more ethnically varied than its neighboring areas. (　)

(2) The magnificent Grand Canyon is located in this region, as is Monument Valley, the starkly beautiful backdrop for many western movies. (　)

(3) The United States obtained Southwest following the Mexican-American War of 1846—1848. All of this land once belonged to Mexico. ( )
(4) Since the last third of the 19th century, the immense stretch of barren American desert has been growing larger. ( )
(5) In the 1860s, the wasteland extended from the Missouri Valley almost to the Pacific Coast. ( )
(6) As they continued to cultivate the desert, its size increased. ( )

The Southwest (Arizona, New Mexico, Oklahoma, Texas) is drier than the **adjoining** Midwest in weather. The population is less dense and, with strong Spanish-American and Native-American components, more ethnically varied than its neighboring areas. Outside the cities, the region is a land of open spaces, much of which is desert. The **magnificent** Grand Canyon is located in this region, as is Monument Valley, the starkly beautiful backdrop for many western movies. Monument Valley is within the Navajo Reservation, home of the most populous American Indian tribe. To the south and east lie dozens of other Indian **reservations**, including those of the Hopi, Zuni, and Apache tribes. Parts of the Southwest once belonged to Mexico. The United States obtained this land following the Mexican-American War of 1846—1848.

The population in the region is growing rapidly. Arizona, for example, now rivals the southern states as a destination for retired Americans in search of a warm climate. Since the last third of the 19th century, the immense stretch of **barren** American desert has been growing smaller. In the 1860s, the wasteland extended from the Mississippi Valley almost to the Pacific Coast. But settlers learned that the prairies could grow corn and that the grasslands could feed cattle and sheep or yield wheat. As they continued to **cultivate** the desert, its size decreased. Dams on the Colorado and other rivers and aqueducts have brought water to the once small towns of Las Vegas, Nevada, Phoenix, Arizona, and Albuquerque, New Mexico, allowing them to become metropolises.

Text C The West

Read the passage about the West quickly. Compare it with other regions in America and finish the multiple-choice questions below.

(1) _____ has a history of European settlement older than that of most Midwestern states.
   A. Wyoming   B. California   C. Montana   D. Colorado

(2) Americans use the undeveloped land of the West for recreational and commercial activities, except _____.
   A. fishing   B. hiking   C. hunting   D. boating

(3) Hawaii is the only state in the union in which _____ are the largest ethnic group.
   A. African Americans   B. Asian Americans
   C. Spanish Americans   D. Mexican Americans

(4) Which of the following words has the same meaning as "live-and-let-live" in the last paragraph?
   A. Tolerant.   B. Gracious.   C. Respectful.   D. Respectable.

(5) Which of the following is NOT true according to the passage?
   A. California has a history of European settlement older than that of most Midwestern states.
   B. Beginning in the 1980s, large numbers of Asians have also settled in Los Angeles. Los Angeles—and Southern California as a whole—bears the stamp of its large Mexican-American population.
   C. Now the second largest city in the nation, Los Angeles is best known as the home of the Hollywood film industry.
   D. Fueled by the growth of Los Angeles and the "Silicon Valley" area near San Jose, California has become the most populous of all the states.

Americans have long regarded the West (Alaska, Colorado, California, Hawaii, Idaho, Montana, Nevada, Oregon, Utah, Washington, Wyoming) as the last frontier. Yet California has a history of European settlement older than that of most Midwestern states. Spanish priests founded **missions** along the California coast a few years before the **outbreak** of the American Revolution. In the 19th century, California and Oregon entered the Union ahead of many states.

The West is a region of scenic beauty on a grand scale. In much of the West, the population is **sparse** and the federal government owns and manages millions of hectares of undeveloped land. Americans use these areas for recreational and commercial activities, such as fishing, camping, hiking, boating, grazing, lumbering, and mining. In recent years, some local residents who earn their livelihoods on federal property have come into conflict with the government agencies, which are charged with keeping land use within environmentally **acceptable** limits.

Hawaii is the only state in the Union in which Asian Americans are the largest **ethnic** group. Beginning in the 1980s, large numbers of Asians have also settled in California. Los Angeles—and Southern California as a whole—bears the stamp of its large Mexican-American population. Now the second largest city in the nation, Los Angeles is best known as the home of the Hollywood film industry. Fueled by the growth of Los Angeles and the "Silicon Valley" area near San Jose, California has become the most populous of all the states. Perhaps because so many westerners have moved there from other regions to make a new start, Western cities are known for their tolerance and a very strong "**live-and-let-live**" attitude.

  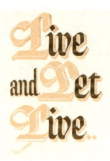

Proper Names

Albuquerque 阿尔伯克基(新墨西哥州第一大城市)
Amherst 阿默斯特(马萨诸塞州一市镇)
Atlanta 亚特兰大(佐治亚州首府及第一大城市)
Dartmouth 达特默思(加拿大东南部城市)
English Protestants 英国新教徒
Las Vegas 拉斯维加斯(内华达州第一大城市,世界著名赌城)
Little Rock 小石城(阿肯色州首府)
Midwesterners 美国中西部居民
Monument Valley 纪念碑谷
New Englanders 新英格兰人
Philadelphia 费城(宾夕法尼亚州第一大城市)
San Jose 圣何塞(加利福尼亚州第三大城市)
Silicon Valley 硅谷
the American Civil War 美国内战
the Apache 阿帕奇(部落)人
the Chesapeake Bay 切萨皮克海湾
the Hollywood 好莱坞
the Hopi 霍皮人
the Mexican-American War 墨美之战
the Mid-Atlantic states 大西洋中部诸州
the Mississippi Valley 密西西比峡谷
the Navajo Reservation 纳瓦霍保护区
the New South 新南方
the Old South 旧南方
the Pacific Coast 太平洋海岸
the Union 联邦
the Zuni 祖尼人
Van Wyck Brooks 范·威克·布鲁克斯(美国文学评论家、历史学家)
Wellesley College 韦尔斯利大学
Wesleyan University 卫斯理大学

For Fun

Works to read

Globalization and Diversity: Geography of a Changing World (2nd Edition)

It is an exciting contemporary approach to World Regional Geography that explicitly acknowledges the geographic changes that accompany today's rapid rate of globalization.

Movies to see

Gone with the Wind

It is a romantic drama and the only novel by Margaret Mitchell. The story follows Scarlett O'Hara, the daughter of a plantation owner in Georgia during and after the Civil War. It is set in Jonesboro and Atlanta during the American Civil War and Reconstruction.

Volcano

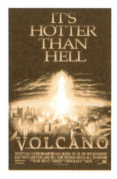

It is a disaster-action film starring Tommy Lee Jones, Anne Heche, and Don Cheadle. It was directed by Mick Jackson, and was released in the United States on April 25, 1997. Filmed in various locations in California, including the Mojave Desert, the city of Torrance, and the Beverly Center, the movie focuses on a volcano which erupts in downtown L.A., threatening to destroy the city.

Once Upon a Time in the West

It is a 1968 epic spaghetti Western film directed by Sergio Leone. The film tells an epic story of a mysterious stranger with a harmonica who joins forces with a notorious desperado to protect a beautiful widow from a ruthless assassin working for the railroad.

The Patriot

It is a 2000 epic war film directed by Roland Emmerich, written by Robert Rodat, and starring Mel Gibson and Heath Ledger. Peaceful farmer Benjamin Martin is driven to lead the Colonial Militia during the American Revolution when a sadistic British officer murders his son.

Songs to enjoy

"The Star-Spangled Banner" by Francis Scott Key

Oh, say, can you see, by the dawn's early light,
What so proudly we hailed at the twilight's last gleaming?
Whose broad stripes and bright stars thru the perilous fight,
O'er the ramparts we watched were so gallantly streaming?
And the rocket's red glare, the bombs bursting in air,
Gave proof through the night that our flag was still there.
Oh, say does that star-spangled banner yet wave
O'er the land of the free and the home of the brave?

On the shore, dimly seen through the mists of the deep,
Where the foe's haughty host in dread silence reposes,
What is that which the breeze, o'er the towering steep,
As it fitfully blows, half conceals, half discloses?
Now it catches the gleam of the morning's first beam,
In full glory reflected now shines in the stream:
'Tis the star-spangled banner! Oh long may it wave
O'er the land of the free and the home of the brave!

And where is that band who so vauntingly swore
That the havoc of war and the battle's confusion,
A home and a country should leave us no more!
Their blood has washed out their foul footsteps' pollution.
No refuge could save the hireling and slave
From the terror of flight, or the gloom of the grave:
And the star-spangled banner in triumph doth wave
O'er the land of the free and the home of the brave!

Oh! thus be it ever, when freemen shall stand
Between their loved home and the war's desolation!
Blest with victory and peace, may the heav'n rescued land
Praise the Power that hath made and preserved us a nation!
Then conquer we must, when our cause it is just,
And this be our motto: "In God is our trust."
And the star-spangled banner in triumph shall wave
O'er the land of the free and the home of the brave!

Appendix 1

USA State Flags

续表

Appendix 2

State Capitals, Largest Cities and Name Origins

State	Capital	Largest City	Name Origin
Alabama	Montgomery	Birmingham	From Alabama River by early European explorers and named "Alibamu" after the local Indian tribe
Alaska	Juneau	Anchorage	Corruption of Aleut word meaning "great land" or "that which the sea breaks against"
Arizona	Phoenix	Phoenix	Uncertain. Perhaps from the O'odham Indian word for "little spring"
Arkansas	Little Rock	Little Rock	From the Quapaw Indians
California	Sacramento	Los Angeles	From a book, Las Sergas de Esplandián, by Garcia Ordóñez de Montalvo, c. 1500
Colorado	Denver	Denver	From the Spanish, "ruddy" or "red"
Connecticut	Hartford	Bridgeport	From an Indian word (Quinnehtukqut) meaning "beside the long tidal river"
Delaware	Dover	Wilmington	From Delaware River and Bay; named in turn for Sir Thomas West, Baron De La Warr
Florida	Tallahassee	Jacksonville	From the Spanish Pascua Florida, meaning "feast of flowers" (Easter)
Georgia	Atlanta	Atlanta	In honor of George II of England
Hawaii	Honolulu	Honolulu	Uncertain. The islands may have been named by Hawaii Loa, their traditional discoverer. Or they may have been named after Hawaii or Hawaiki, the traditional home of the Polynesians.
Idaho	Boise	Boise	An invented name whose meaning is unknown.
Illinois	Springfield	Chicago	Algonquin for "tribe of superior men"
Indiana	Indianapolis	Indianapolis	Meaning "land of Indians"
Iowa	Des Moines	Des Moines	From the Iowa River which was named after the Ioway Indian tribe
Kansas	Topeka	Wichita	From a Sioux word meaning "people of the south wind"
Kentucky	Frankfort	Lexington	From an Iroquoian word "Ken-tah-ten" meaning "land of tomorrow"
Louisiana	Baton Rouge	New Orleans	In honor of Louis XIV of France

续表

Maine	Augusta	Portland	First used to distinguish the mainland from the offshore islands. It has been considered a compliment to Henrietta Maria, queen of Charles I of England. She was said to have owned the province of Mayne in France.
Maryland	Annapolis	Baltimore	In honor of Henrietta Maria (queen of Charles I of England)
Massachusetts	Boston	Boston	From Massachusett tribe of Native Americans, meaning "at or about the great hill"
Michigan	Lansing	Detroit	From Indian word "Michigana" meaning "great or large lake"
Minnesota	St. Paul	Minneapolis	From a Dakota Indian word meaning "sky-tinted water"
Mississippi	Jackson	Jackson	From an Indian word meaning "Father of Waters"
Missouri	Jefferson City	Kansas City	Named after the Missouri Indian tribe. "Missouri" means "town of the large canoes."
Montana	Helena	Billings	From the Spanish word meaning "mountain"
Nebraska	Lincoln	Omaha	From an Oto Indian word meaning "flat water"
Nevada	Carson City	Las Vegas	Spanish："snowcapped"
New Hampshire	Concord	Manchester	From the English county of Hampshire
New Jersey	Trenton	Newark	From the Channel Isle of Jersey
New Mexico	Santa Fe	Albuquerque	From Mexico, "place of Mexitli," an Aztec god or leader
New York	Albany	New York City	In honor of the Duke of York
North Carolina	Raleigh	Charlotte	In honor of Charles I of England
North Dakota	Bismarck	Fargo	From the Sioux tribe, meaning "allies"
Ohio	Columbus	Columbus	From an Iroquoian word meaning "great river"
Oklahoma	Oklahoma City	Oklahoma City	From two Choctaw Indian words meaning "red people"
Oregon	Salem	Portland	Unknown. However, it is generally accepted that the name, first used by Jonathan Carver in 1778, was taken from the writings of Maj. Robert Rogers, an English army officer.

续表

Pennsylvania	Harrisburg	Philadelphia	In honor of Adm. Sir William Penn, father of William Penn. It means "Penn's Woodland."
Rhode Island	Providence	Providence	From the Greek Island of Rhodes
South Carolina	Columbia	Columbia	In honor of Charles I of England
South Dakota	Pierre	Sioux Falls	From the Sioux tribe, meaning "allies"
Tennessee	Nashville	Memphis	Of Cherokee origin; the exact meaning is unknown.
Texas	Austin	Houston	From an Indian word meaning "friends"
Utah	Salt Lake City	Salt Lake City	From the Ute tribe, meaning "people of the mountains"
Vermont	Montpelier	Burlington	From the French "vert mont," meaning "green mountain"
Virginia	Richmond	Virginia Beach	In honor of Elizabeth "Virgin Queen" of England
Washington	Olympia	Seattle	In honor of George Washington
West Virginia	Charleston	Charleston	In honor of Elizabeth, "Virgin Queen" of England
Wisconsin	Madison	Milwaukee	French corruption of an Indian word whose meaning is disputed
Wyoming	Cheyenne	Cheyenne	From the Delaware Indian word, meaning "mountains and valleys alternating"; the same as the Wyoming Valley in Pennsylvania

Appendix 3

Fifty States, Nick Names and Fun Facts

State	Nick Names	Information
Alabama	Yellowhammer State	George Washington Carver, who dis-covered more than 300 uses for peanuts
Alaska	The state is commonly called "The Last Frontier" or "Land of the Midnight Sun"	The longest coastline in the US, 6,640 miles, greater than that of all other states combined
Arizona	Grand Canyon State	The most telescopes in the world, in Tucson
Arkansas	The Natural State	The only active diamond mine in the US
California	Golden State	"General Sherman," a 3,500-year-old tree, and a stand of bristlecone pines 4,000 years old are the world's oldest living things
Colorado	Centennial State	The world's largest silver nugget (1,840 pounds) found in 1894 near Aspen
Connecticut	Constitution State (official, 1959); Nutmeg State	The first American cookbook, published in Hartford in 1796: American Cookery by Amelia Simmons
Delaware	Diamond State; First State; Small Wonder	The first log cabins in North America, built in 1683 by Swedish immigrants
Florida	Sunshine State (1970)	US spacecraft launchings from Cape Canaveral, formerly Cape Kennedy
Georgia	Peach State, Empire State of the South	The Girl Scouts, founded in Savannah by Juliette Gordon Low in 1912
Hawaii	Aloha State (1959)	The only royal palace in the US (Iolani)
Idaho	Gem State	The longest main street in America, 33 miles, in Island Park
Illinois	Prairie State	The tallest building in the US, Sears Tower, in Chicago
Indiana	Hoosier State	The famous car race: the Indy 500
Iowa	Hawkeye State	The shortest and steepest railroad in the US, Dubuque: 60° incline, 296 feet
Kansas	Sunflower State; Jayhawk State	Helium discovered in 1905 at the University of Kansas

		续表
Kentucky	Bluegrass State	The largest underground cave in the world: 300 miles long, the Mammoth-Flint Cave system
Louisiana	Pelican State	The most crayfish: 98% of the world's crayfish
Maine	Pine Tree State	The most easterly point in the US, West Quoddy Head
Maryland	Free State; Old Line State	The first umbrella factory in the US, 1928, Baltimore
Massachusetts	Bay State; Old Colony State	The first World Series, 1903: the Boston "Americans" (became the Red Sox in 1908) vs. the Pittsburg Pirates (Pittsburgh had no "h" between 1890—1911)
Michigan	Wolverine State	The Cereal Bowl of America, Battle Creek, produces most cereal in the US
Minnesota	North Star State; Gopher State; Land of 10,000 Lakes	The oldest rock in the world, 3.8 billion years old, found in Minnesota River valley
Mississippi	Magnolia State	Coca-Cola, first bottled in 1894 in Vicksburg
Missouri	Show-me State	Mark Twain and some of his characters, such as Tom Sawyer and Huckleberry Finn
Montana	Treasure State	Grasshopper Glacier, named for the grasshoppers that can still be seen frozen in ice
Nebraska	Cornhusker State (1945); Beef State	The only roller skating museum in the world, in Lincoln
Nevada	Sagebrush State; Silver State; Battle Born State	Rare fish such as the Devils Hole pup, found only in Devils Hole, and other rare fish from prehistoric lakes; also the driest state
New Hampshire	Granite State	Artificial rain, first used near Concord in 1947 to fight a forest fire
New Jersey	Garden State	The world's first drive-in movie theater, built in 1933 near Camden
New Mexico	Land of Enchantment (1999)	"Smokey Bear," a cub orphaned by fire in 1950, buried in Smokey Bear Historical State Park in 1976
New York	Empire State	The first presidential inauguration: George Washington took the oath of office in New York City on April 30, 1789.
North Carolina	Tar Heel State	Virginia Dare, the first English child born in America, on Roanoake Island in 1587

续表

North Dakota	Sioux State; Flickertail State; Peace Garden State; Rough Rider State	The geographic center of North America, in Pierce County, near Balta
Ohio	Buckeye State	The first electric traffic lights, invented and installed in Cleveland in 1914
Oklahoma	Sooner State	The first parking meter, installed in Oklahoma City in 1935
Oregon	Beaver State	The world's smallest park, totaling 452 inches, created in Portland on St. Patrick's Day for leprechauns and snail races
Pennsylvania	Keystone State	The first magazine in America: the American Magazine, published in Philadelphia for 3 months in 1741
Rhode Island	The Ocean State	Rhode Island Red chickens, first bred in 1854; the start of poultry as a major American industry
South Carolina	Palmetto State	The first tea farm in the US, created in 1890 near Summerville
South Dakota	Mount Rushmore State; Coyote State	The world's largest natural, indoor warmwater pool, Evans' Plunge in Hot Springs
Tennessee	Volunteer State	Graceland, the estate and gravesite of Elvis Presley
Texas	Lone Star State	NASA, in Houston, headquarters for all piloted US space projects
Utah	Beehive State	Rainbow Bridge, the largest natural stone bridge in the world, 290 feet high, 275 feet across
Vermont	Green Mountain State	The largest production of maple syrup in the US
Virginia	The Old Dominion; Mother of Presidents	The only full-length statue of George Washington, placed in capitol in 1796
Washington	Evergreen State	Lunar Rover, the vehicle used by astronauts on the moon; Boeing, in Seattle, makes aircraft and spacecraft
West Virginia	Mountain State	Marbles; most of the country's glass marbles made around Parkersburg
Wisconsin	Badger State	The typewriter, invented in Milwaukee in 1867
Wyoming	Equality State	The "Register of the Desert," a huge granite boulder covering 27 acres with 5,000 early pioneer names carved on it

Appendix 4

States by Order of Entry into Union

State	Entered Union	Year Settled
1. Delaware	Dec. 7, 1787	1638
2. Pennsylvania	Dec. 12, 1787	1682
3. New Jersey	Dec. 18, 1787	1660
4. Georgia	Jan. 2, 1788	1733
5. Connecticut	Jan. 9, 1788	1634
6. Massachusetts	Feb. 6, 1788	1620
7. Maryland	Apr. 28, 1788	1634
8. South Carolina	May 23, 1788	1670
9. New Hampshire	June 21, 1788	1623
10. Virginia	June 25, 1788	1607
11. New York	July 26, 1788	1614
12. North Carolina	Nov. 21, 1789	1660
13. Rhode Island	May 29, 1790	1636
14. Vermont	Mar. 4, 1791	1724
15. Kentucky	June 1, 1792	1774
16. Tennessee	June 1, 1796	1769
17. Ohio	Mar. 1, 1803	1788
18. Louisiana	Apr. 30, 1812	1699
19. Indiana	Dec. 11, 1816	1733
20. Mississippi	Dec. 10, 1817	1699
21. Illinois	Dec. 3, 1818	1720
22. Alabama	Dec. 14, 1819	1702
23. Maine	Mar. 15, 1820	1624
24. Missouri	Aug. 10, 1821	1735
25. Arkansas	June 15, 1836	1686
26. Michigan	Jan. 26, 1837	1668
27. Florida	Mar. 3, 1845	1565
28. Texas	Dec. 29, 1845	1682
29. Iowa	Dec. 28, 1846	1788

续表

30. Wisconsin	May 29, 1848	1766
31. California	Sept. 9, 1850	1769
32. Minnesota	May 11, 1858	1805
33. Oregon	Feb. 14, 1859	1811
34. Kansas	Jan. 29, 1861	1727
35. West Virginia	June 20, 1863	1727
36. Nevada	Oct. 31, 1864	1849
37. Nebraska	Mar. 1, 1867	1823
38. Colorado	Aug. 1, 1876	1858
39. North Dakota	Nov. 2, 1889	1812
40. South Dakota	Nov. 2, 1889	1859
41. Montana	Nov. 8, 1889	1809
42. Washington	Nov. 11, 1889	1811
43. Idaho	July 3, 1890	1842
44. Wyoming	July 10, 1890	1834
45. Utah	Jan. 4, 1896	1847
46. Oklahoma	Nov. 16, 1907	1889
47. New Mexico	Jan. 6, 1912	1610
48. Arizona	Feb. 14, 1912	1776
49. Alaska	Jan. 3, 1959	1784
50. Hawaii	Aug. 21, 1959	1820

Appendix 5

State Birds and State Flowers

State	State Bird	Image	State Flower	Image
Alabama	Yellowhammer a.k.a. Northern Flicker		Camellia (state flower)	
	Wild Turkey (state game bird)		Oak-leaf Hydrangea (state wildflower)	
Alaska	Willow Ptarmigan		Forget-me-not	
Arizona	Cactus Wren		Saguaro Cactus blossom	
Arkansas	Mockingbird a.k.a. Northern Mockingbird		Apple blossom	
California	California Quail		California Poppy	
Colorado	Lark Bunting		Rocky Mountain Columbine	

续表

Connecticut	American Robin		Mountain laurel	
Delaware	Blue Hen of Delaware		Peach blossom	
District of Columbia	Wood Thrush		American Beauty Rose	
Florida	Mockingbird		Orange blossom	
Georgia	Brown Thrasher (state bird)		Cherokee Rose (state flower)	
Georgia	Bobwhite Quail (state game bird)		Azalea (state wildflower)	
Hawaii	Nene or Hawaiian Goose		Hawaiian hibiscus (ma'o hau hele)	
Idaho	Mountain Bluebird		Mock Orange	

续表

Illinois	Cardinal aka Northern Cardinal		Violet	
Indiana	Cardinal		Peony	
Iowa	Eastern Goldfinch a.k.a. American Goldfinch		Wild Prairie Rose	
Kansas	Western Meadowlark		Sunflower	
Kentucky	Northern Cardinal		Goldenrod	
Louisiana	Eastern Brown Pelican		Magnolia (state flower)	
			Louisiana Iris (state wildflower)	
Maine	Black-capped Chickadee		White pine cone and tassel	

续表

Maryland	Baltimore Oriole		Black-eyed susan	
Massachusetts	Black-capped Chickadee		Mayflower	
	Wild Turkey (state game bird)			
Michigan	American Robin		Apple blossom (state flower)	
			Dwarf Lake Iris (state wildflower)	
Minnesota	Common Loon		Pink and white lady's slipper	
Mississippi	Mockingbird		Magnolia (state flower)	
	Wood duck (state waterfowl)		Tickseed (state wildflower)	
Missouri	Eastern Bluebird		Hawthorn	

Montana	Western Meadowlark		Bitterroot	
Nebraska	Western Meadowlark		Goldenrod	
Nevada	Mountain Bluebird		Sagebrush	
New Hampshire	Purple Finch		Purple lilac	
New Jersey	Eastern Goldfinch		Violet	
New Mexico	Roadrunner a.k.a. Greater Roadrunner		Yucca flower	
New York	Eastern Bluebird		Rose	
North Carolina	Cardinal		Flowering Dogwood	

续表

North Dakota	Western Meadowlark		Wild Prairie Rose	
Ohio	Cardinal		Scarlet Carnation (state flower)	
			Large white trillium (state wild flower)	
Oklahoma	Scissor-tailed Flycatcher		Oklahoma Rose (state flower)	
			Mistletoe (state floral emblem)	
			Indian Blanket (state wildflower)	
Oregon	Western Meadowlark		Oregon grape	
Pennsylvania	Ruffed Grouse		Mountain Laurel (state flower)	
			Penngift Crown Vetch (beautification and conservation plant)	

Rhode Island	Rhode Island Red Chicken		Violet	
South Carolina	Mockingbird (former state bird)		Yellow Jessamine	
	Carolina Wren		Goldenrod (state wildflower)	
	Wild Turkey (state wild game bird)			
South Dakota	Ring-necked Pheasant		Pasque flower	
Tennessee	Mockingbird		Iris	
	Bobwhite Quail (state wild game bird)		Passion flower (state wildflower)	
Texas	Mockingbird		Bluebonnet	
Utah	California Gull		Sego lily	

续表

Vermont	Hermit Thrush		Red Clover	
Virginia	Cardinal		American Dogwood	
Washington	Willow Goldfinch a.k.a. American Goldfinch		Coast Rhododendron	
West Virginia	Cardinal		Rhododendron	
Wisconsin	American Robin		Wood Violet	
Wyoming	Western Meadowlark		Indian Paintbrush	

Appendix 6

State Areas

Rank	state/territory	total (sq mi)	(km^2)	land (sq mi)	(km^2)	water (sq mi)	(km^2)	% water
1	Alaska	663,267	1,717,854	571,951	1,481,346	91,316	236,507	13.77
2	Texas	268,581	695,622	261,797	678,051	6,784	17,570	2.53
3	California	163,696	423,971	155,959	403,932	7,736	20,036	4.73
4	Montana	147,042	380,837	145,552	376,978	1,490	3,859	1.01
5	New Mexico	121,589	314,914	121,356	314,311	234	606	0.19
6	Arizona	113,998	295,253	113,635	294,313	364	943	0.32
7	Nevada	110,561	286,352	109,826	284,448	735	1,904	0.66
8	Colorado	104,094	269,602	103,718	268,628	376	974	0.36
9	Oregon	98,381	254,806	95,997	248,631	2,384	6,175	2.42
10	Wyoming	97,814	253,337	97,100	251,488	713	1,847	0.73
11	Michigan	96,716	250,493	56,804	147,122	39,912	103,372	41.27
12	Minnesota	86,939	225,171	79,610	206,189	7,329	18,982	8.43
13	Utah	84,899	219,887	82,144	212,752	2,755	7,135	3.25
14	Idaho	83,570	216,445	82,747	214,314	823	2,132	0.98
15	Kansas	82,277	213,096	81,815	211,900	462	1,197	0.56
16	Nebraska	77,354	200,346	76,872	199,098	481	1,246	0.62
17	South Dakota	77,116	199,730	75,885	196,541	1,232	3,191	1.60
18	Washington	71,300	184,666	66,544	172,348	4,756	12,318	6.67
19	North Dakota	70,700	183,112	68,976	178,647	1,724	4,465	2.44
20	Oklahoma	69,898	181,035	68,667	177,847	1,231	3,188	1.76
21	Missouri	69,704	180,533	68,886	178,414	818	2,119	1.17
22	Florida	65,755	170,305	53,927	139,670	11,828	30,634	17.99
23	Wisconsin	65,498	169,639	54,310	140,662	11,188	28,977	17.08
24	Georgia	59,425	153,910	57,906	149,976	1,519	3,934	2.56
25	Illinois	57,914	149,997	55,584	143,962	2,331	6,037	4.02

续表

26	Iowa	56,272	145,744	55,869	144,700	402	1,041	0.71
27	New York	54,556	141,299	47,214	122,284	7,342	19,016	13.46
28	North Carolina	53,819	139,391	48,711	126,161	5,108	13,230	9.49
29	Arkansas	53,179	137,733	52,068	134,856	1,110	2,875	2.09
30	Alabama	52,419	135,765	50,744	131,426	1,675	4,338	3.20
31	Louisiana	51,840	134,265	43,562	112,825	8,278	21,440	15.97
32	Mississippi	48,430	125,433	46,907	121,489	1,523	3,945	3.15
33	Pennsylvania	46,055	119,282	44,817	116,075	1,239	3,209	2.69
34	Ohio	44,825	116,096	40,948	106,055	3,877	10,041	8.65
35	Virginia	42,774	110,784	39,594	102,548	3,180	8,236	7.43
36	Tennessee	42,143	109,150	41,217	106,752	926	2,398	2.20
37	Kentucky	40,409	104,659	39,728	102,895	681	1,764	1.68
38	Indiana	36,418	94,322	35,867	92,895	551	1,427	1.51
39	Maine	35,385	91,647	30,862	79,932	4,523	11,715	12.78
40	South Carolina	32,020	82,931	30,109	77,982	1,911	4,949	5.97
41	West Virginia	24,230	62,755	24,078	62,362	152	394	0.63
42	Maryland	12,407	32,134	9,774	25,315	2,633	6,819	21.22
43	Hawaii	10,931	28,311	6,423	16,635	4,508	11,676	41.24
44	Massachusetts	10,555	27,337	7,840	20,306	2,715	7,032	25.72
45	Vermont	9,614	24,900	9,250	23,957	365	945	3.79
46	New Hampshire	9,350	24,216	8,968	23,227	382	989	4.08
47	New Jersey	8,721	22,587	7,417	19,210	1,304	3,377	14.95
48	Connecticut	5,543	14,356	4,845	12,548	699	1,810	12.60
49	Delaware	2,489	6,446	1,954	5,061	536	1,388	21.52
50	Rhode Island	1,545	4,002	1,045	2,707	500	1,295	32.37
51	District of Columbia	68	176	61	158	7	18	10.16
52	Puerto Rico	5,325	13,792	3,425	8,871	1,900	4,921	35.68

续表

53	Northern Mariana Islands	1,975	5,115	179	464	1,796	4,652	90.93
54	US Virgin Islands	737	1,909	134	347	604	1,564	81.87
55	American Samoa	584	1,513	77	199	506	1,311	86.75
56	Guam	571	1,479	210	544	361	935	63.22
	US Minor Outlying Islands	16	41	16	41	0	0	0.00
	50 states + DC	3,794,083	9,826,630	3,537,438	9,161,922	256,645	664,707	6.76
	all US territory	3,803,290	9,850,476	3,541,479	9,172,389	261,811	678,087	6.88

Appendix 7

重点参考书目和网站

[1] Akin, W. E. (1968). *The North Central United States*. Princeton: D. Van Nostrand Company, Inc.
[2] Birdsall, Stephen S. & Florin J. (1992). *An Outline of American Geography: Regional Landscapes of the United States*. New York: John Wiley & Sons, Inc.
[3] Blacklock, L. (1974). The High West. New York City: Viking Press. Inc.
[4] Estall, R. (1972). *A Modern Geography of the United States: Aspects of Life and Economy*. New York City: Quadrangle/The New York Times Co.
[5] Findley, R. (1972). *Great American Deserts*. Washington D. C.: National Geographic Society.
[6] Goodwyn, L. (1967). *The South Central States: Arkansas, Louisiana, Oklahoma, Texas*. New York City: Time-Life Books.
[7] Jones, E. (1968). *The Plains States: Iowa, Kansas, Minnesota, Missouri, Nebraska, North Dakota, and South Dakota*. New York City: Time-Life books.
[8] Leacock, E. (2002). *Travels Across America*. Washington, D.C.: National Geographic Society.
[9] McCarthy, J. (1967). *The Heartland: Illinois, Indiana, Michigan, Ohio, Wisconsin*. New York City: Time-Life Books.
[10] Mittleman, E. N. (1986). *An Outline of American Geography*. Washington: United States Information Agency.
[11] Morgan, N. B. (1967). *The Pacific States: California, Oregon, Washington*. New York City: Time-Life Books.
[12] Osborne, J. (1968). *The Old South: Alabama, Florida, Georgia, Mississippi, South Carolina*. New York City: Time-Life Books.
[13] Shein, S. & Ashcrogt, M. (2003). *North America*. Washington, D.C.: National Geographic Society.
[14] Smith, R. A. (1968). *The Frontier States: Alaska, Hawaii*. New York City: Time-Life Books.
[15] Sprague, M. (1967). *The Mountain States: Arizona, Colorado, Idaho, Montana, Nevada, New Mexico, Utah, Wyoming*. New York City: Time-Life Books.
[16] Williams, R. L. (1973). *The Northwest Coast*. New York City: Time-Life Books.
[17] 陈立凯. (2007) 美国风情: 地理与文化[M]. 南京: 南京大学出版社.
[18] 美国国家地理学会. (2004) 美国之旅教师指导与评估手册[Z]. 北京: 外语教学与研究出版社.
[19] 伊斯比. (2006) 今日美国[M]. 任小池, 张红春注. 北京: 外语教学与研究出版社.
[20] 余耀生, 郁明亮. (1997) 美国风光揽胜[M]. 张小玲编译. 上海: 东方出版中心.
[21] 周敏, 沈明德. (2002) 美国一览[M]. 北京: 中国地图出版社.
[22] Bear River Course Geologic Backgrounds: http://esp.cr.usgs.gov/info/lacs/rivercourse.htm.
[23] Biography Search Guide: http://www.123exp-biographies.com/t/00034112106/.
[24] Boyzone Lyrics: http://www.mp3lyrics.org/b/boyzone/melting-pot/.
[25] Bureau of International Information Programs, US Department of State, (1997). *Portrait of the USA: From Sea to Shining Sea*, http://beijing.usembassy-china.org.cn/usintro.html.
[26] Bureau of International Information Programs, US Department of State, (1998). *Outline of American Geography*, http://beijing.usembassy-china.org.cn/usintro.html.
[27] Bureau of International Information Programs, US Department of State, (2005). *See You in the USA*, http://beijing.usembassy-china.org.cn/usintro.html.
[28] Free Encyclopedia: http://en.wikipedia.org/wiki.
[29] Geography of San Francisco: http://geography.howstuffworks.com/united-states/geography-of-san-francisco.htm/printable.

[30] Globalization and Diversity: http://www.sciencedaily.com.
[31] Internet Movie Data Basis: http://www.imdb.com.
[32] Lyrics Freak: http://www.lyricsfreak.com.
[33] Music Videos and Lyrics: http://www.musicloversgroup.com/emigrate-new-york-city-lyrics-and-video/.
[34] National Geographic Society, US Map with Links to State Maps: http://beijing.usembassy-china.org.cn/usintro.html.
[35] National Geography Magazine: http://ngm.nationalgeographic.com/.
[36] Paul Goldberger Quotes: http://en.thinkexist.com.
[37] Professional Travel Guide: http://www.professionaltravelguide.com/.
[38] Sports Logos: http://www.sportslogos.net/.
[39] The Great Lyrics Provider: http://www.lyricstime.com.
[40] United States Geography: http://encarta.msn.com.
[41] US National Park Service: http//www.nps.gov/grba/planyourvisit/the-great-basin.htm.
[42] USA and State Flag: http://www.enchantedlearning.com.